Sustainable Housing Design Guide for Scotland

Fionn Stevenson
Nick Williams

> **Did You Know?**
>
> - the use of trees and planting can save up to 5% on tenants' energy bills
>
> - the use of sunshine collected in dwellings can save up to 15% on tenants' energy bills
>
> - Painting as a trade is carcinogenic and professional painters have a lung cancer rate 40% above the average.
>
> - PVC is restricted in use in several European countries due to its potentially harmful environmental effects
>
> - the use of additional insulation in housing developments can achieve substantial energy savings for very little extra cost
>
> - there are a variety of alternatives to toxic timber treatments including no treatment at all
>
> - there may be over 250 different chemicals emitting fumes in a typical new kitchen
>
> - re-used timber can be of superior quality to new timber

Scottish Homes
THE NATIONAL HOUSING AGENCY

SCOTTISH
NATURAL
HERITAGE

D1341161

©The Stationery Office 2000

All rights reserved. No part of this publication may be reproduced, stored in a retrieval system, or transmitted in any form or by any means, electronic, mechanical, photocopying, recording or otherwise without the permission of the publisher.

Applications for reproduction should be made in writing to The Stationery Office Limited, St Crispins, Duke Street, Norwich NR3 1PD.

The information contained in this publication is believed to be correct at the time of manufacture. Whilst care has been taken to ensure that the information is accurate, the publisher can accept no responsibility for any errors or omissions or for changes to the details given.

A CIP catalogue record of this book is available from the British Library.
A Library of Congress CIP catalogue record has been applied for.

First published 2000
ISBN 0 11 4972796

Contents

* Chapters 3 to 6 relate to new build, maintenance and rehabilitation

Acknowledgements

The Sustainable Housing Design Guide for Scotland was commissioned by Scottish Homes and written by Fionn Stevenson and Nick Williams and illustrated by Julie Macrae.

The authors would like to acknowledge the assistance given by the following in the production of this Design Guide.

Steering Group

Neil Ferguson	Scottish Homes
Misia Jack	Scottish Federation of Housing Associations
Liz McLean	East Lothian Council
James Shirazi	Scottish Homes
Ian Walker	Scottish Homes

Staff from a number of housing associations in Scotland were also involved in the development of the Design Guide and the authors would like to thank them for their contribution.

The production of this publication was made possible with the additional support of Scottish Natural Heritage.

"Housing, and settlement design, have a key role to play in moving towards a sustainable Scotland. The issues here are not only about resource use. Having attractive and secure places to live and take leisure is a prerequisite of making settlements places where people want to spend their time. Scottish Natural Heritage welcomes the messages within this publication and supports the long-term objective of a better quality of life for all."

John Markland, Chairman
Scottish Natural Heritage

Acronyms

AECB	Association for Environment Conscious Building
BRE	Building Research Establishment
BRECSU	Building Research Establishment Central Support Unit
BREDEM	Building Research Establishment Domestic Energy Model
BREEAM	Building Research Establishment Environmental Assessment Method
CAT	Centre for Alternative Technology
CHP	combined heat and power
DETR	Department of the Environment, Transport and the Regions
DH	district heating
DoE	Department of the Environment
DPH	dwellings per hectare
EMF	electromagnetic field
ETSU	Energy Technology Support Unit
HRH	habitable rooms per hectare
HDRA	Henry Doubleday Research Association
HMSO	Her Majesty's Stationery Office
LCA	life cycle analysis
LCC	life cycle costing
LPA	local planning authority
NHBC	National House Building Council
NHER	National Home Energy Rating
NPPG	National Planning Policy Guideline
PAN	Planning Advice Note
PSV	passive stack ventilation
RCEP	Royal Commission on Environmental Pollution
RICS	Royal Institute of Chartered Surveyors
RSL	Registered Social Landlord
SAP	Standard Assessment Procedure
SEPA	Scottish Environmental Protection Agency
SFHA	Scottish Federation of Housing Associations
uPVC	unplasticized polyvinyl chloride
VOC	volatile organic compound

Introduction

Sustainable development means economic prosperity and security, enhanced social welfare and social inclusion, and a healthy natural environment. These are all connected; success in one policy area is dependent on success in others. Successive UK Governments have recognised the importance of sustainable development to quality of life and the achievement of policy objectives across a wide range of issues[1]. This will have important implications for all those involved in housing in Scotland and will require placing sustainability at the heart of housing practice. This has been recognised by Scottish Homes in their Sustainable Development Policy[2] which aims to encourage, support and fund development that is more sustainable in terms of its production and use, and to facilitate a change of culture which puts the concept of sustainability centre stage.

Against this background this design guide is intended to provide comprehensive and user friendly guidance to the incorporation of sustainability principles into maintaining, rehabilitating and developing housing.

Sustainable Housing Performance Assessment

In order to help developers assess the extent to which they are incorporating sustainability into their activities, Scottish Homes has also financed the production of a Housing Quality Assessment Program which has been published at the same time as this guide. The Guide and the Housing Quality Assessment Program are complementary and should be used together.

---

[1] Department of the Environment, Transport and the Regions (1999)
[2] Scottish Homes (2000)

How to use this guide

This guide is not a detailed technical manual, but a first source to consult for housing providers who wish to move toward more sustainable development. Comprehensive references and a bibliography are provided from which detailed technical information can be obtained.

We strongly encourage Registered Social Landlords (RSLs) to adapt their own design guides to incorporate the principles contained in this guide (see Box 3.1).

Some RSLs in Scotland have already begun to move toward more sustainable housing. The benefits of their experience have been incorporated in this guide in an Appendix as case studies for use by others.

The Guide has been broken down for convenience into separate chapters dealing with specific issues of sustainability and housing. It is vitally important to appreciate however that all these issues are connected and it makes little sense to deal with them in isolation in real developments. Developers should use all of the guide when planning actual developments. The gains made from building energy efficient dwellings can be lost, for example, if they are built in a location remote from public transport and their residents are as a consequence highly car dependent.

Chapter One explains how housing can both make a contribution to the achievement of sustainability objectives, and also benefit itself in terms of quality, performance and value for money by incorporating sustainable design principles.

Chapter Two deals with those aspects of sustainability connected with the location, form and function of residential developments considered as a whole. This covers land use planning, transport, social cohesion and community issues.

Chapters Three to Seven deal with the functional design of dwellings. This covers the systematic environmental evaluation of dwellings, including energy and physical resource efficiency, and health issues. Chapter Seven deals specifically with rehabilitation and maintenance issues.

Chapter Eight examines the financial and management implications of sustainable housing design, including procurement and life cycle costing.

Chapter One
Sustainability And Housing

The characteristics of our built environment are vital to the achievement of sustainability objectives. These include cutting greenhouse gas emissions, reductions in pollution and the conservation of resources, cohesive and inclusive communities, and a prosperous and secure economy. Housing in particular can make a significant contribution to sustainability because:

- it consumes large amounts of resource in its construction, maintenance and use
- it is a fixed asset with a long life and
- it is central to quality of life and has implications beyond housing affecting transport, health, employment and community.

The relationship between sustainability and housing is two-way. Incorporating principles of sustainability into housing development, maintenance and refurbishment will not only make a significant contribution to the achievement of general sustainability objectives, but will also provide important advances in the quality, durability and cost effectiveness of our housing.

There is a need for a **change of culture** with regard to housing development which places sustainability centre stage. This should include the developers (be they housing associations or for-profit companies), builders and land use planners and also the tenants and owners. Sustainability objectives will be achieved only if they are taken into account at all stages from design through construction to long term use and eventual disposal and recycling. Raising of awareness is important for all those involved.

1.1

How Housing Can Contribute To Sustainability

1.1.1 Minimising climate change

Did you know?
Housing in Scotland emits almost 18 million tonnes of CO_2 each year. This is about 30% of all CO_2 emissions.

The most widespread and potentially damaging environmental problem at present is global climate change as a result of the emission of greenhouse gases, notably CO_2. The scientific consensus is that Scotland is expected to become windier and wetter, and that temperatures in Scotland will not rise as fast as in the south east of England. Gale frequencies over the country may increase by up to 30% by the year 2050[1]. This would be damaging to agriculture and the tourist industry and increase the risks of flooding. An alternative possibility is that the Gulf Stream may shift away from the British Isles bringing much colder and drier climatic conditions; this would also damage agriculture and increase demand for energy. As a result of the Kyoto Conference and the subsequent meeting in Buenos Aires, the UK Government has agreed to a legally binding international commitment to reduce emissions of the six main greenhouse gases by 12.5% compared to 1990 during the five-year period 2008-2012, and in addition an objective to cut 1990 level CO_2 emissions by 20% by 2010.

The main means of achieving these targets will be in the transport sector, notably by decreasing travel in general and car use in particular[2]. The housing sector also has an important role to play, both in terms of dwelling characteristics and the structure and location of residential developments. Housing consumes large quantities of energy in its production and use:

- between 40 and 50% of UK CO_2 emissions are attributable to buildings, two thirds of this to the domestic sector
- 10 per cent of UK CO_2 emissions are due to embodied energy used in the construction process
- Scottish housing emits 17.8 million tonnes of CO_2 per annum, an average of 8.5 tonnes per dwelling.

This is particularly important in Scotland given the severity of the climate and the poor performance of the existing housing stock. The 1996 Scottish House Condition Survey[3] revealed that:

- less than 10% of Scottish dwellings meet the modest standards of energy efficiency set by the current building regulations (a National Home Energy Rating of about 7)
- the average NHER for the stock as a whole was only 4.1
- 11,000 Scottish housing association dwellings had poor NHERs of 0, 1 or 2 (although overall housing association dwellings performed better than other tenures).

---

[1] Department of the Environment, Transport and the Regions (1998a)
[2] RCEP (1994)
[3] Scottish Homes (1997)

This is wasteful of energy and offers considerable potential for reducing greenhouse gas emissions through improvements in the energy efficiency of the Scottish housing stock. The Home Energy Conservation Act has set a target of a 30% reduction in home energy use which if achieved would represent approximately 7.5% of all emissions and a substantial part of the UK Government's target of 12.5 per cent.

1.1.2 Reducing the need for physical resources

In the UK as a whole, the construction industry uses six tonnes of material per person per year, which on a pro rata basis gives an annual total for Scotland of over 30 million tonnes.

Improvements in the way we design and build our dwellings offer opportunities to use materials more sparingly. At the end of a building's life, recycling and re-use would reduce the need for quarrying and other source activities and also the amount of landfill required on demolition. Only one per cent of construction material is re-used in Scotland and there are large sustainability gains to be made in terms of resource consumption and environmental impact through better practice. This includes refurbishment of existing buildings as well as greater use of recycled and re-used materials.

1.1.3 Reducing pollution and improving air quality and health

In addition to greenhouse gases energy use in the home produces other gases which have negative effects. These include SO_2 (which causes acid rain), NO_x and CO (which are poisonous). Greater levels of energy efficiency will reduce the output of these pollutants. A combination of more airtight buildings and the increasing use of synthetic materials has resulted in a collection of ill health effects known as sick building syndrome resulting from indoor air pollution. These include headaches, nausea, eye and skin irritations and breathing difficulties. Careful choice of building materials can boost the use of renewable resources which reduces pollution levels both indoors and outdoors.

1.1.4 Creating sustainable settlements

The single biggest source of greenhouse gases is the transport sector and these particular emissions can be significantly reduced by planning and building in such a way that travel is reduced, and where necessary can be achieved by walking, cycling or public transport. Housing should be located close to employment and services and also to public transport. The co-operation of housing developers, land use planners and transport planners will be crucial to ensure that we build in such a way that accessibility is maximised and car dependency minimised. This has been spelt out in the Government's recent Scottish White Paper on integrated transport[4]. This will mean departing from old conventional wisdoms about the form of the built environment; building at higher densities will be preferable

---

[4] Scottish Office (1998b)

to lower densities and mixed land uses will be preferred to single use zoning.

The number of households in Scotland is projected to increase by 250,000 by 2010 and this will create pressure on housing and land supply[5]. It is therefore important to make the maximum use of the land resources available. Building at higher densities will contribute but we will also require the use of greenfield sites to be minimised and brownfield sites to be maximised. Guidance has been issued to this effect[6]. In parts of Scotland at present up to 70% of new housing has been built on brownfield sites and this figure should be achieved more widely. More effective use can also be made of land and building resources by refurbishing existing buildings (including non-residential buildings) for new dwellings where this is cost effective.

> **Did you know?**
> More than 90% of Scottish dwellings do not meet the minimum energy efficiency standard set out in the Building Regulations.

1.2

How Sustainable Development Benefits Housing

The previous sections described how housing can contribute to the achievement of sustainable development objectives. This is a two-way process because the most cost-effective way to develop and maintain a high quality housing stock in the long term is to incorporate principles of sustainability into all parts of the housing development process. Since new build comprises only a small fraction of the existing stock it is also important that refurbishment incorporates sustainability principles.

1.2.1 Energy efficiency

The poor performance of the Scottish housing stock in terms of energy efficiency is not only wasteful of resources and the cause of harmful pollution, but also a contributory cause of poverty and poor health and is particularly damaging in Scotland because of the severe climate, especially in northern and exposed areas.

Higher energy efficiency can make a significant difference to quality of life, health and material standard of living, especially to poor households. Many Scottish households cannot afford to heat their houses properly, or go without other essentials to do so. A quarter of Scottish dwellings suffer from condensation or dampness, in part because of inadequate heating. This has well established harmful effects on health[7] and imposes an additional burden on deprived households. The improvement of domestic energy efficiency for lower income households can potentially enable them to heat their homes to a higher standard, reduce condensation and dampness, and release income for other purposes. It can make significant contributions to enhanced health and reduced poverty. Many Scottish Registered Social Landlords are addressing issues of fuel poverty by building to standards of insulation much higher than

---

[5] Wilcox, S. et al (1998)
[6] Scottish Office (1996)
[7] Scottish Office (1999b)

determined by the Building Regulations.

1.2.2 Social inclusion

The problems of the large peripheral schemes of our major cities are testament to the importance of building communities rather than merely groupings of dwellings. A sustainable housing development would not only have environment friendly and energy efficient buildings, it would also have access to employment, schools, shops, places of entertainment, primary health care, and it would be accessible by public transport. It would also be mixed in terms of tenures, incomes and age groups. For a house to be a home it must be geographically located such that its inhabitants can use it as a base from which to enter society at large; it must facilitate social inclusion and not be a mechanism of social exclusion as much Scottish housing has been in the past.

Scale is an important dimension of sustainability. Housing developments should not be so large that they alienate the people who live in them. Residents should be given the opportunity to take responsibility for their environment whether they are tenants or owner occupiers, and this is only possible when they live in developments or management units which are small enough for this to be practicable.

Residential development which is designed to contribute to sustainability will provide not only warm, dry and healthy homes and reduce the need to travel, but also a setting which enhances quality of life from generation to generation and which integrates people into society at large. It will maximise the effectiveness of housing investment and be crucial to the building of cohesive communities.

1.2.3 Value for money and economic effectiveness

Making economies in the short term can often lead to poor value for money in the long term. Building cheaply may produce more dwellings for money spent, but in the long term may cost more. The essence of sustainability is a consideration of long term costs and benefits. Residential development according to sustainability principles may cost more in the short term, but will have a significant downward effect on overall, long term costs.

Extra expenditure on energy efficiency, for example, may increase capital costs but there is evidence that in the long term the savings in running costs will exceed the initial extra capital costs[8]. There is also evidence that building to a high environmental specification leads to lower maintenance and management costs[9]. Whole life costing can be used to estimate long term costs and allocate them to different people and agencies (landlord, tenant, developer). These techniques are essential to the effective application of sustainability to

[8] Ecologica Ltd (1996)
[9] Energy Efficiency Office (1993, 1994)

residential development and are explored in more detail in
Chapter 8.

People's housing needs change as they age. It makes sense to
produce homes which have flexible physical structures so that
they can be adapted to changing uses over time. This may
mean that people can stay in their homes longer, or that
dwellings and residential areas generally can house different
people over time. Planning for the long term - planning for
sustainability - can increase the flexibility and effectiveness of
the housing stock and lower long term costs. Guidance has
already been issued on how to provide for housing of varying
needs in a flexible manner[10].

The remainder of this design guide provides information on
how to incorporate sustainability into housing development in
Scotland and provides reference to sources from which more
detail can be obtained. It also includes case studies of
environmentally friendly housing developments in Scotland and
incorporates the experience gained from these developments.

---

[10] Stationery Office (1999)

Chapter Two
Planning, Community And Sustainability

This Chapter deals with how to make residential developments more sustainable when considered as a whole and within the wider context of the built environment, urban and rural. The focus will be on the role of housing providers in the development process, including the redevelopment of existing areas, within a land use planning and urban design system which gives sustainability a prime position.

2.1

What Makes Residential Development Sustainable?

A sustainable residential development

* minimises resource use, waste and pollution
* provides the physical context for a cohesive community and
* provides access to employment.

Satisfying all these requirements can be achieved by moving towards a different urban form which challenges the accepted wisdom of land use planning in the post war era. Higher density, mixed use development can reduce the need for travel, make better use of existing urban space and infrastructure, and provide high quality residential areas. In rural areas, development in existing settlements can also reduce the need for travel (although to a lesser extent than in urban areas) and makes maximum use of existing infrastructure. The ways in which sustainability can be achieved are summarised in Table 2.1 and described below.

2.1.1 Resource use and pollution

The biggest source of pollution from residential neighbourhoods, urban and rural, is car use. A key dimension of neighbourhood sustainability is the extent to which travel to and from the neighbourhood is minimised and opportunities for walking, cycling and the use of public transport are maximised.

Given the rising demand for housing generated by falling household size and other demographic changes, increasing pressure will be placed on land for residential development.

The form and location of development will have implications for travel patterns, car use and levels of pollution. Resource use can be reduced by making the maximum use of existing infrastructure and land.

These issues can be tackled and neighbourhood sustainability enhanced by:

- mixed land use development
- higher residential densities
- use of brownfield sites
- lower levels of parking provision, including car-free development
- residential development designed to enhance walking, cycling and the use of public transport.

Higher densities and mixed use development can also reduce non-transport energy consumption, in particular heating and power requirements. Combined heat and power (CHP) and district heating (DH) schemes become more viable with higher densities and mixed uses (see Chapter Four).

Table 2.1 Neighbourhood sustainability

PROBLEMS	CAUSES	SOLUTIONS	MECHANISMS
Energy use (transport) Pollution	Car dependency	Reduce need to travel Facilitate other travel modes	Mixed land uses Higher densities Access to public transport Car free developments Home zones Pedestrian friendly design Cycleways
Energy use (heat and power) Pollution	Inefficient heating systems	More efficient heating systems	Combined heat and power District heating Neighbourhood design
Land take/ infrastructure use	Greenfield development Low densities	Brownfield development Higher densities	Brownfield development Higher densities
Social exclusion	Segregation Single tenure development Unequal access to facilities Remoteness from centres of employment	Social mix Equal access to facilities Accessibility to employment centres	Mixed tenure development Changed allocation policies Equal access to facilities Siting of housing close to employment Foyers Use of local labour

2.1.2 A cohesive community

Making towns and cities, especially their inner areas and peripheral schemes, more attractive as places to live is both an essential part of urban regeneration and also an opportunity for residential development to become more sustainable (Figures 2.1 - 2.2). This covers not only the environmental dimension but also the social aspects of sustainability in terms of cohesive neighbourhood communities. The most energy efficient and environment friendly neighbourhood possible is useless if people don't want to live in it. Fortunately, it is possible to develop and redevelop in such a way that environmental and social dimensions reinforce each other.

Ideally, settlements in rural areas and neighbourhoods in urban areas should be communities. Community as a concept is difficult to define and even more difficult to put into practice; there are no magic formulae to produce communities. It is possible however to say what successful communities should be like. They should be secure and crime free, offer access to schools, shops, entertainment and employment, and facilitate the creation and maintenance of supportive social networks. To avoid the large scale social polarisation so evident in parts of Scotland, they should wherever possible be mixed in tenure, income levels, family types and age groups. As many of these elements as possible should be present. Research has revealed for example that mixed tenure alone does not increase social interaction within a neighbourhood[1]. As a minimum, cohesive communities require:

- continuity and a low turnover of residents
- social balance
- high quality urban design.

Figure 2.1 A typical historical urban settlement which by its nature is people friendly. This stems from the requirement there has been for interaction and activity at street level. (after Rudlin and Falk)

Figure 2.2 A scene which is typical of many contemporary developments, where housing is inward looking and priority is given over to the car and other modes of vehicular traffic. (after Rudlin and Falk)

---

[1] Scottish Homes (1998a)

2.1.3 Residential development and jobs

The location of residential development so that it is accessible to employment is an essential component of sustainability; it reduces travel and pollution, strengthens local economies and counters social exclusion. Large areas of low demand for housing have been created at least partly because of a lack of access to employment; this is wasteful of resources and socially harmful.

Integrating employment and housing provision is not easy, however, since they are normally the responsibility of different agencies. Direct ways of ensuring that jobs and homes are integrated include foyers (where accommodation for young people is linked to training[2]) and the use of local labour in housing redevelopment[3]. More generally, housing providers should always consider the access to employment when planning development for households of working age.

2.2

Achieving Neighbourhood Sustainability

As the rate of replacement of the housing stock is about one per cent per annum, achieving neighbourhood sustainability becomes a task of working with the existing built environment rather than optimising the opportunities presented by new build on a large scale. This implies accommodation and compromise. Housing providers have to work with the development opportunities, especially sites that arise.

Moreover, housing is just one element of a neighbourhood and housing developers must work with others - local authorities, the private sector, and other voluntary organisations - if co-ordinated and successful sustainability strategies are to be achieved. This means that partnerships are essential if neighbourhood sustainability is to be enhanced.

2.2.1 Sustainability and the planning system

A sustainable neighbourhood has essential elements which are not the responsibility of housing developers and over which they have little influence. Overall control of neighbourhood development lies mainly with land use planners, who determine crucial variables such as land use mix and residential densities. Planning for much of the post war period was driven by accommodation of the car (minimum parking standards for residential development for instance), low densities (below 20 dwellings per hectare in many cases), and mono-functional zoning of land use. Since the UK Government's commitment to sustainable development following the Earth Summit in Rio in 1992, however, planning policies have been radically revised and detailed guidance is now available to local planning

---

[2] Scottish Homes (1998b)
[3] Scottish Homes (1998c)

authorities on how to incorporate sustainability into development plans[4]. Specific guidance has also been issued for Scotland through National Planning Policy Guidelines and Planning Advice Notes. Of particular relevance are NPPG 3 "Land for Housing", and NPPG 17 and PAN 57 "Transport and Planning" (see Box 2.1)[5]

Box 2.1
Scottish Office guidance on planning and sustainability

The following have been advocated by the Scottish Office:

- the re-use of urban land (NPPG 3, paragraph 13)
- using existing infra-structure to the full (NPPG 3, paragraph 18)
- taking into account the energy efficiency of the settlement patterns (NPPG 3, paragraph 18)
- re-use of existing buildings (NPPG 3, paragraph 25)
- mixed use development (NPPG 3, paragraph 28)
- where new settlements are necessary they should be readily serviced by public transport (NPPG 3, paragraph 44)
- where development is necessary in the countryside, it should preferably be infill development or extensions to existing villages, or conversions of existing buildings (NPPG 3, paragraph 52)
- the setting of maximum, not minimum parking standards (NPPG 17, paragraphs 21 and 22)
- the co-ordination of housing densities with transport provision (NPPG 17, paragraph 29)
- car free developments (PAN 57, paragraph 46)

As a result new planning policies to achieve sustainability can be at variance in some areas with approved development plans. It is possible that a developer's application or proposals for a sustainable residential development will not conform to the approved development plan when this has not been recently revised although it is worth noting that, under certain circumstances, NPPG1 explicitly permits developments contrary to approved development plans[6].

The biggest obstacle to maximising sustainability, however, is that housing providers must work with the opportunities that arise. The Government has issued guidance that local planning authorities should favour a **sequential approach** to development whereby developers are required to consider sustainability as a priority when evaluating developments and sites[7]. This means developing sites which can deliver sustainable development in advance of alternative sites, for example developing brownfield sites before greenfield sites (Figure 2.3). RSLs rarely if ever have the luxury of a range of sites from which to choose for development and a sequential evaluation of a number of sites in terms of meeting

---

[4] Department of the Environment, Transport and the Regions (1998b)
[5] Scottish Office (1996, 1999c and 1999d)
[6] Scottish Office (1994a) paragraphs 64-69
[7] Department of the Environment, Transport and the Regions (1998b)

sustainability objectives is rarely possible. RSLs must work with the sites that become available when they become available.

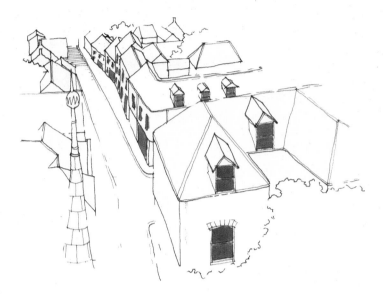

Figure 2.3 Maximising urban density, through developing brownfield sites over greenfield sites. (after Rudlin and Falk)

Nevertheless, housing providers can look for sites which offer opportunities for sustainable development and develop those sites which do become available in sustainable ways.

Discussion with local planning authorities on how this can be done will aid the development process and developers should attempt to incorporate the Scottish Office guidance given in Box 2.1 into their development programme wherever possible. It can be assumed that development proposals which enhance sustainability will be considered more favourably by planning authorities than those which do not[8].

2.2.2 Mixed land uses

Mixed land use developments have the potential to

- reduce travel by bringing different activities closer together
- revitalise an area formerly dominated by only one activity
- increase neighbourhood safety and security
- enhance sense of place and quality of life, especially for the elderly and non-mobile
- increase access to employment

---

[8] A comprehensive and detailed guide to all the issues discussed in this chapter is given in Barton et al (1995). Land use planning issues are covered comprehensively in DETR (1998b). Although produced by DETR this deals with issues relevant to Scotland and includes Scottish examples.

RSLs can become involved in mixed use development in a variety of ways:

- by developing housing in areas with no existing residential property (either new build or redevelopment, e.g. conversion of the upper floors of commercial or retail buildings). This need not require partnerships with other agencies but may require challenging an existing local development plan (Figure 2.4). The Merchant City in Glasgow is a former commercial area which has become mixed use as a result of private residential development and conversion of warehousing to residential use
- by developing more than one activity in a single building (e.g. Perthshire Housing Association's property in Scott Street, Perth where the Association's offices are on the ground floor of their own flatted development; also East Lothian Housing Association and Partick Housing Association have property with workspaces on the ground floor and housing on upper floors)
- by becoming involved in non-residential as well as residential development. Queens Cross Housing Association has established sister organisations to develop workshop and office accommodation within the Association's geographic area of operation. Although not linked to specific housing developments, attempts are made to lease the premises to businesses connected to the Association's activities such as repair and maintenance. Moreover, sites unsuitable for housing development have been used for some of the workshops and offices

Did you know?
Tesco and the Peabody Trust have built a joint development with a foodstore on the ground floor and over 100 flats above.

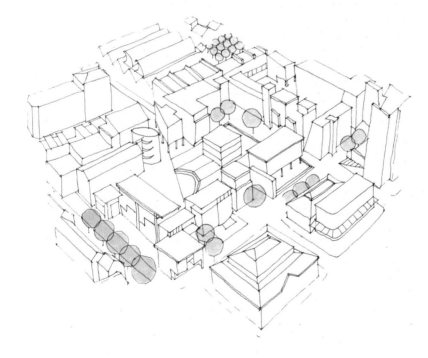

Figure 2.4 Successful mixed use development at Smithfield, Manchester, which accommodates almost 250 residential units and provides commercial space at ground and first floor levels. (after Rudlin and Falk)

- by becoming involved in comprehensive regeneration projects which are designed to produce mixed use development. The Crown Street Regeneration Project for the Gorbals, in Glasgow has produced residential, retail, entertainment and office space; some of the residential properties are being developed by the New Gorbals Housing Association (see Case Study 1).

More detailed guidance on mixed use development can be found in *Making Places: a Guide to Good Practice in Undertaking Mixed Use Development Schemes* (English Partnerships and Urban Villages Forum 1998)[9].

2.2.3 Residential densities

Increasing residential densities can:

- reduce land take (most significantly when moving from 20 to 40 dwellings per hectare)
- reduce travel and enhance the viability of public transport
- increase opportunities for non-transport energy saving (for example by making CHP possible)
- reduce the space required for roads and car parking and make development more pedestrian friendly
- enhance the viability of existing or potential facilities by increasing numbers of people within walking distance.

The DETR[10] guidance on density suggests using dwellings per hectare (DPH) for estimating development land requirements, and habitable rooms per hectare (HRH) at the site-specific level. The latter allows for greater flexibility in finding the best solution for a particular site (e.g. flats or houses) (Figures 2.5 - 2.8). No single figure can be given as the correct net residential density, but densities of over 70 DPH have been achieved in the Crown Street Regeneration Project in Glasgow and higher densities than this are compatible with quality residential environments with careful design. Densities of 40-50 DPH (225-275 HRH) should be easily obtainable without damaging residential quality in most circumstances (current suburban densities are 20 DPH or lower in many areas). Most RSLs in Scotland are already building at high density because of land costs, but the environmental advantages of doing so should not be ignored. This illustrates how environmental considerations and cost effectiveness reinforce one another.

The following should also be noted:

- higher density itself is not sufficient and must be accompanied by other design standards (such as lower parking provision, preservation of open space and high building quality)
- higher densities do not mean "town cramming" and should be accompanied by good urban design (see Section 2.2.7)

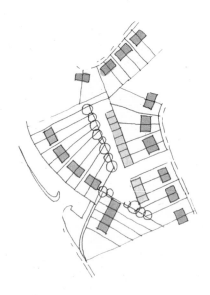

Did you know?
Residential densities of over 70 dwellings per hectare will be achieved in the Crown Street Regeneration Project.

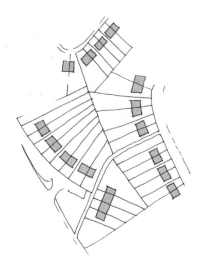

Figure 2.5 Existing backland opportunity to increase density on site. (after Rudlin and Falk)

Figure 2.6 Backland infill providing 11 additional residential units without overcrowding plot. (after Rudlin and Falk)

---

[9] See also Aldous (1992); Rowley (1996, 1998); and Roger Tym and Partners (1991)
[10] Department of the Environment, Transport and the Regions (1998b, 1998c)

- they can be achieved without recourse to high rise development
- where a local plan which has not been recently revised to take account of sustainability objectives is prescriptive with regard to density, discussions should take place with the LPA as to the potential for increasing the density allowed
- densities should be varied according to local conditions
- the unthinking application of high densities can make development less sustainable. The highest density development should be located around traffic nodes and accessible to public transport. High densities remote from public transport merely increase the numbers of people who are car dependent. Similarly, high density residential development remote from existing infrastructure and other land uses increases the need for extra expenditure and resource use on new infrastructure. Wherever possible high density development should take advantage of existing spare capacity.

More detailed guidance is available in the DETR documents *The Use of Density in Urban Planning and Planning for Sustainable Development: Toward Better Practice*, Chapter 2 See also guidance from Llewelyn-Davies (1994 and 1998)[11].

2.2.4 Brownfield sites

The use of brownfield sites:

- reduces demand for green field land
- enhances the viability of public transport
- makes maximum use of existing infrastructure
- increases overall urban densities and the viability of existing services
- offers opportunities for high quality residential development in terms of increased access to jobs, shops and other services
- provides the potential for innovation, such as car free development.

Brownfield sites are not restricted to urban areas and should also be used in rural areas when available and appropriate. Redundant airfields or hospitals for instance can be used for residential development as long as other sustainability principles are satisfied. Not all brownfield sites will be suitable for residential use (for example where public transport is absent) and difficulties may be presented such as land contamination and fragmented land ownership. These may make a sequential procedure of site evaluation in which brownfield sites are examined before greenfield development difficult given the constraints of a development programme, but RSLs should be positive in their attitude to brownfield development.

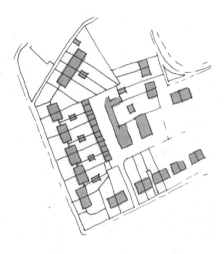

Figure 2.7 Redundant garages and courts offer an opportunity to increase density on site. (after Rudlin and Falk)

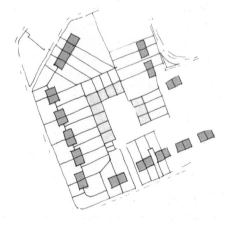

Figure 2.8 After clearance an infill provides 11 additional residential units without overcrowding plot. (after Rudlin and Falk)

---

[11] Llewelyn-Davies (1994, 1998)

2.2.5 Transport considerations

A sustainable neighbourhood should reduce the need to travel; where travel is necessary opportunities to walk, cycle and use public transport should be maximised. Walking and cycling in particular should be encouraged. This not only reduces pollution but is also an important element of building community cohesion; a neighbourhood within which people feel comfortable walking will facilitate more social interaction.

Mixed land uses and higher residential densities have already been mentioned as helpful in reducing overall travel and facilitating walking, cycling and public transport (Figures 2.9 - 2.10). Sites which have poor access to public transport should not be developed unless it will be provided in the near future. In addition, developers should consider the following as development options:

- decrease the amount of space within developments for vehicles and maximise space for pedestrians; pavements should be widened and roads narrowed
- the setting of maximum rather than minimum parking standards
- car free developments where appropriate (for example in central locations where high quality public transport is available and access to employment, shops and other facilities is possible by walking or cycling)
- establishment of home zones - residential developments within which strict controls are placed on vehicles (for example a very low speed limit such as 10 mph). This creates a residential environment within which public space is more user friendly in general and child friendly in particular. Nine pilot home zones have been established in England.[12]

Figure 2.9 A community with distinct but disconnected developments. (after Rudlin and Falk)

2.2.6 Community and sustainability

Community cohesion is a vital element of neighbourhood sustainability and has been damaged in the past by social polarisation and tenure segregation. RSLs provide mainly for those on low incomes or who are vulnerable in some other way. It is important that residential provision for these groups occurs in such a way that they are integrated into the broader community. Mixed communities can be encouraged by:

- mixed tenure developments
- allocation systems for rented accommodation which place less emphasis on housing need.

RSLs may wish to consider these as options within their general development programme. Either option can be used or both. A partnership with a private developer in which the former builds dwellings for sale while an RSL builds rented accommodation within the same area would enable the RSL to continue to

Figure 2.10 Repairing the disconnected community with careful infill development. (after Rudlin and Falk)

---

[12] More information can be obtained from *At home in my street: exploring home zones in the Netherlands and Germany*, a video produced for Transport 2000 and the Children's Play Council.

prioritise housing need in their allocations and produce mixed neighbourhoods.

2.2.7 Urban and neighbourhood design

The elements of sustainable residential development have been described in the preceding sections. Whether a particular development succeeds or not depends in part on how these different elements are put together, in other words on high quality urban design. This has tended to be neglected in the past, especially outside central city areas. Moreover developers, including RSLs, have devoted most of their attention to dwelling design and paid less attention to overall neighbourhood design and quality (Figures 2.11 - 2.13). The quality of public space is as important as private space in determining the success of our neighbourhoods and settlements. It is important that all developers understand what contributes to good urban design. When designing their own development, they should take into account its context and the manner in which it relates to other adjacent developments and activities. Some broad principles of good urban design produced by the Urban and Economic Development Group are shown in Box 2.2[13], and a Scottish example of careful urban design is given in Case Study 1.

Figure 2.11 Traditional massing creates visual diversity through incorporating a variety of building types and heights.

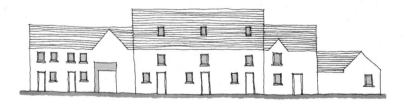

Figure 2.12 Contemporary massing reduces cohesion and minimises visual interest.

---

[13] Further guidance on urban design can be found on the web site *Resource for Urban Design Information* (http://rudi.herts.ac.uk/rudi.html). This has links to a variety of design guides including the *Essex Design Guide for Residential and Mixed Use Areas* (Essex Planning Officers' Association 1998) and *Time for Design 2: Good Practice in Building, Landscape and Urban Design* (English Partnerships 1998). The Scottish Office has also issued guidance on how to fit new housing into the landscape in both rural and urban areas. For urban areas see PAN 44 *Fitting New Housing into the Landscape*, and for rural areas see PAN 36 *Siting and Design of New Housing in the Countryside*. Guidance on greenspace in residential development can be found in the CD-ROM *Quality Greenspace for Residential Areas* produced by Scottish Natural Heritage, Scottish Homes, COSLA and the Scottish Housebuilders' Association

Figure 2.13 In contemporary society opportunities for social interaction are often reduced.

Box 2.2 Principles of urban design

Quality space – a high quality urban environment created by well proportioned buildings and attractive, well maintained spaces. This public realm is human in scale but urban in nature and designed to promote interaction and to accommodate the diversity of urban life.

A framework of streets and squares – An urban structure based upon a clear network of streets and public squares designed to serve both as routes and as public places supervised by the occupants of surrounding buildings.

A rich mix of uses – A diversity of uses, buildings and tenures accommodated within a common street pattern. This reduces commuting and car travel to facilities as well as fostering activity and greater security throughout the day and a more balanced community.

A critical mass of activity – A density of uses to create sufficient activity and people to animate streets and public places and to sustain shops and other public facilities.

Minimal environmental harm – The development of urban areas which are sustainable both in terms of their environmental impact and in their ability to be flexible and adapt to future changes. This includes good public transport, waste recycling, combined heat and power, well insulated housing, urban ecology, water saving and sustainable materials.

Integration and permeability – A framework of streets to provide a degree of permeability giving a choice of routes and making the area feel safer. Successful urban areas avoid the development of housing and workspace as defined estates but rather mix them up and blur the boundaries between them.

A sense of place – The use of landmarks, vistas and focal points along with the incorporation of existing features and buildings or imaginative landscaping and public art to give new urban areas a unique character and memorability.

FROM URBED WEB SITE:
http://www.urbed.co.uk/sun/design-principles.html

2.2.8 Rural Areas

Although the principles of sustainability are the same in both rural and urban areas, practical ways of achieving sustainability objectives will differ. In particular, the potential for reducing travel in rural areas through residential development is significantly less than in urban areas.

Nevertheless, the Scottish Office has recommended that where development is necessary in the countryside, it should preferably be infill development or extensions to existing villages, or conversions of existing buildings[14]. This will have some effect on reducing travel where development takes place in or adjacent to existing settlements but more significantly will make the maximum use of existing land and building resources. Guidance has also been issued stating that where new settlements are necessary they should be readily serviced by public transport[15].

2.2.9 Partnership

For a housing provider to play a full part in achieving sustainable neighbourhoods, it may have to co-operate with a variety of organisations. As well as the planning authority, partners are likely to include other public sector bodies, voluntary and private sector agencies, and not least local residents themselves[16]. Sustainable housing development reinforces the wider action agenda for housing which recognises the links between housing and health, education and employment, which in turn depend on the co-operation and partnership of a range of delivery agencies.

Partnerships operate at a range of spatial scales, from inter - authority to neighbourhood levels[17]. As far as sustainability is concerned, RSLs can become involved with other bodies at two levels:

- at the local authority level by contributing to Local Agenda 21 strategies and Community Plans[18]. This will involve helping local authorities with the development of general strategies rather than specific projects

- at neighbourhood level by developing specific projects designed to contribute to sustainability objectives. Attempts should be made to involve those who will be living in and adjacent to the proposed development.

An example of a partnership which is delivering sustainable development is the Homes for the Future project, a mixed tenure, brownfield residential development adjacent to Glasgow Green. This involves the Glasgow Development Agency, Scottish Homes, the Wise Group (employment training agency), Thenew Housing Association and four private developers.

---

[14] Scottish Office (1996) paragraph 52

[15] Scottish Office (1996) paragraph 44

[16] Scottish Homes (1995)

[17] Scottish Homes (1999b)

[18] Scottish Office (1998c)

Chapter Three
The Site And The Dwelling

When taken together, **site, resources, energy and health** are inseparable aspects of design consideration with each affecting the other. As a result, each aspect should always be considered in relation to the others. For the sake of convenience, however, it is useful to refer to these headings individually. The following four chapters deal with these four different aspects of dwelling design and cover all types of housing activity. Chapter Seven summarises aspects that are uniquely related to maintenance and rehabilitation.

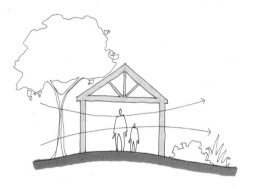

Figure 3.1 The standard house still allows resources to be used up and thrown away; very little is recycled.

Box 3.1	The Principles of sustainable design for dwellings

1. HOLISTIC APPROACH - An integrated design approach is preferable to a fragmented one; everything is connected to everything else

2. SITE -The specific nature of a place controls sustainable design

3. ENERGY USE - Reducing energy use is more cost effective than producing or reclaiming it

4. RESOURCE USE – Aiming for durability and re-use is more efficient than recycling products and materials

5. HEALTH - A sustainable environment is a healthy one for people

6. SIMPLICITY - Simple solutions are better than those which are complicated, over-designed or rely on "technical fixes"

7. EFFICIENCY - Good sustainable design produces multiple benefits from one feature

8. PARTICIPATION - Sustainable design involves the user at all stages

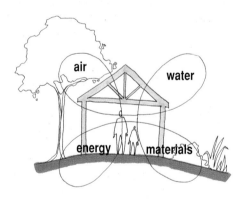

Figure 3.1a "The whole house" acts as a recycling system in carefully re-using all of the elements wherever possible. This helps maximise the efficiency of resource use (after GAIA architects).

Climate And Orientation

Climate is a key factor in sustainable design and its variation (Figures 3.2 - 3.3) has great influence on the effectiveness of housing in terms of social activity, human comfort, health, physical resource use and energy use. The correct orientation of housing layouts and the plan of the individual dwelling will ensure an optimal response to the climate (see Section 3.1.1 and Box 3.2). Even in existing housing or tight urban locations where orientation is restricted, it is still possible to significantly improve the response of the dwelling to the climate (see Section 3.1.2).

The four key site variables in the Scottish climate for optimising sustainable design are:

- Solar Energy

- Wind

- Precipitation

- Temperature

3.1.1 Solar Energy: maximising passive solar gain

Scotland has ample sunshine to make its use worthwhile in a variety of ways in housing for heating purposes. The heating season in Scotland is longer than in England which makes the use of solar energy more cost effective in Scotland than in England in terms of reducing heating bills[1]. Even on cloudy days approximately 30% of solar radiation can be usefully harnessed for lighting and energy use.

The following benefits can be obtained from using solar energy:

- the building form itself can capture solar energy for heating and save around 10-15% on annual heating costs

- mechanical systems which capture solar energy for the heating of hot water can save up to 50% on annual hot water costs (see Table 4.3)

- both passive and active modes of solar heating can be retrofitted to old stock

- active solar water heating using solar water panels has an average financial payback of 10 years, well within the life of the panel itself (see Table 4.3)

- retro-fitted sunspaces (Figures 3.5 - 3.10) can save energy and offer an additional low cost amenity space for three seasons of the year.

---

[1] Bartholomew, DML. (1984)

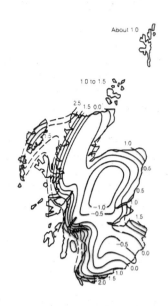

Figure 3.2 Scottish minimum average annual temperature in January.

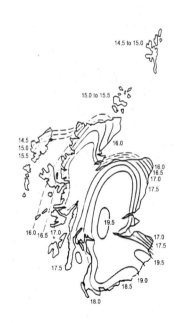

Figure 3.3 Maximum average annual temperature in July showing a wider variation.

Passive solar gain is the use of solar energy for heating by using the dwelling layout and form to capture and store the sun's heat for use both in the day and evening[2]. Ideally, housing should lie roughly on an east/west axis with habitable rooms to the south (Figure 3.4). This layout is not always possible due to planning constraints, but should be adopted wherever practical.

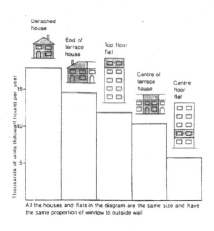

Did you know?
In one monitored retrofitted solar scheme in Scotland heating bills were reduced from £15-£23 a week to an average of £3-£6 a week

Figure 3.4A This chart demonstrates the relative amount of energy used each year by different house types.
Source: GLC (Greater London Council)

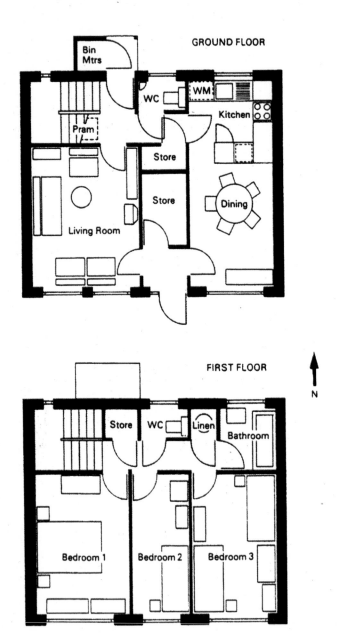

Figure 3.4 A typical passive solar house plan
Source: Brian Edwards.

---

[2] There are a number of publications on passive solar which give guidance on passive solar design in housing : BRECSU has published several free reports BRECSU (1997), BRECSU GPG79, BRECSU (1994b). More technical detail is offered by Energy Research Group (1994), Lowe, R, et al (1996). A good introductory and highly illustrated book is Energy Research Group (1996).

The main method of capturing and storing solar energy is through large south facing windows situated in a highly insulated dwelling but an additional means is through using sunspaces. These are highly glazed south facing amenity areas or porches which are either added or incorporated in to the dwelling layout to enhance passive solar gain and reduce heat loss. There are four ways in which sunspaces save energy:

- Thermal Buffering

- Pre-heated Ventilation

- Draught lobby

- Evening heating

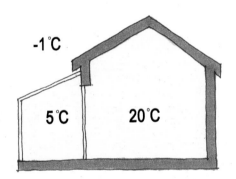

Figure 3.5 Thermal Buffering: by acting as an intermediate heating zone, sunspaces provide an additional insulation layer to walls and windows. (After Borer and Harris, 1998)

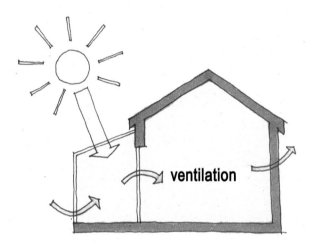

Figure 3.6 Pre-heated Ventilation: fresh air can be pre-warmed by sunspaces before it enters the house via windows, doors and ventilators. (After Borer and Harris, 1998)

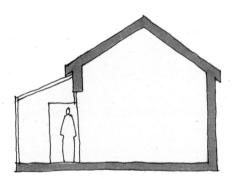

Figure 3.7 Draught lobby: by acting as an air-lock when external doors are opened, sunspaces used as porches reduce ventilation heat loss. (After Borer and Harris, 1998)

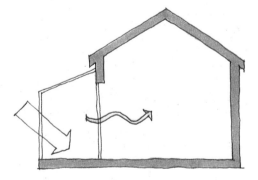

Figure 3.8 Evening heat: by storing and re-radiating heat stored in solid walling solar sunspaces can continue to provide warmth in the evenings once outside temperatures have cooled. (After Borer and Harris, 1998)

Energy gathered during the day will be lost in the evening, if sunspaces are not effectively insulated from the outside. It is a matter of training the occupier to ensure that any shutters or insulated blinds in sunspaces are closed at night to prevent heat loss. Airways through doors, windows or ventilators between the sunspace and living area should also be closed off once it is apparent that the sunspace is cooler than the living area.

Passive solar gain methods must also be established in tandem with daylighting design in order to ensure optimum performance (see Section 4.2.2). There are a number of methods and tools available to help carry out these calculations. One of the best known is BREDEM[3]. Method 5000[4] is a simpler version. There are also numerous "shareware" solar gain tools on the internet[5].

Careful siting of deciduous trees can stop overheating of south facing rooms and conservatories in the summer with full leaf shade, while allowing more light to penetrate in the winter due to less foliage. Care must be taken not to over shade with trees as even in winter deciduous trees can take away up to 50% of daylight when densely planted (Figure 3.11).

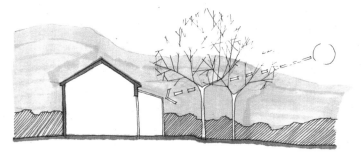

Figure 3.11 Siting of trees relative to the house is critical to ensure that sun can still penetrate into the building. If trees are too close overshadowing will occur (After Borer and Harris, 1998).

> **Did you know?**
> Passive solar energy can provide up to 25% of the heating requirements for an ordinary family house.

Figure 3.9 James Nisbet Street, Glasgow before re-furbishment showing open balconies.

Figure 3.10 James Nisbet Street after retrofit to introduce sun spaces to the block using existing balcony structure.

---

[3] BREDEM (Building Research Establishment Domestic Energy Model) is available from BRE and is designed to calculate heating demands on the basis of gains and losses, using computer software. BRE (1995)
[4] Method 5000 is a manual tool and is found in Energy Research Group (1994)
[5] e.g. http://ourworld.compuserve.com/homepages/dacPc/solacalc.htm

Box 3.2 **Passive solar gain: pointers for good practice**

- site layout should provide access to sunshine for as many dwellings as possible and avoid overshading (see figure 3.12)
- housing layouts should be orientated within 30 degrees of due south wherever possible in order for the solar gain to be useful
- plan cooler service spaces on the north side and habitable rooms needing warmth on the south side
- make sure the building is well insulated and relatively airtight
- allow for adequate and controllable ventilation to avoid overheating in summer
- incorporate draught lobbies to minimise heat loss
- glazing should be optimised with a 70:30 ratio of glazing from south to north elevations to maximise passive solar gain
- provide thermal mass where possible to absorb solar gain (up to 100mm blockwork is effective) and avoid overheating
- the use of conservatories or sunspaces purely for energy reasons is not effective unless they are a cheap, unheated, preferably single glazed (which uses considerably less material resources than double glazing and doesn't rely on vulnerable sealants), three season amenity space
- narrow width sunspaces (under 1500 mm wide) are preferable to room sized ones or conservatories to prevent them from being treated as an additional room and being heated
- provide full separation and insulation between sunspaces and the main dwelling
- provide structural overhangs, external shutters and internal blinds to prevent both overheating in summer and heat loss at night
- cover as much of the south facing wall as practical with a sunspace to act as a thermal buffer
- use deciduous trees and planting to provide partial shade to sunspaces in the summer

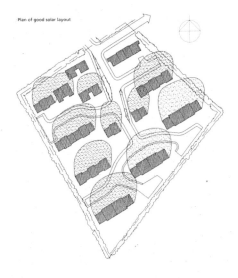

Plan of good solar layout

Figure 3.12 Plan of solar layout showing shadows cast by housing which define space to be left between houses.

3.1.2 Wind: Design With Form, Layout And Land Cover

Even if an urban development site does not offer much opportunity for passive solar gain, all housing can benefit from design for shelter as wind chill contributes significantly to energy loss. Generally, the best orientation for solar gain is also the best for preventing heat loss due to prevailing wind chill from the southwest and north east (Figure 3.13). Regional wind data can be obtained from the Meterological Office[6] but site measurements and analysis will give a more accurate picture for design purposes[7].

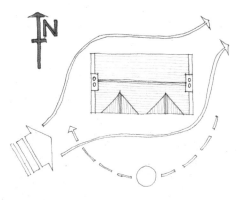

Figure 3.13 The house which presents the narrow end to prevailing winds also maximises the opportunity for passive solar gain (After Borer and Harris, 1998).

[6] HMSO ,The Climate of Scotland: some facts and figures, Edinburgh
[7] BRE (1990a)

27

Housing form can reduce the effect of windchill and heat loss. The ideal form for housing will minimise surface area for heat loss but retain surface variation and texture to increase wind drag. One of the most energy efficient forms of housing is the tenement block. Terraced two storey housing is also very effective. The least effective are the semi-detached and detached house (Figure 3.14 and Figure 3.4A). Providing external structures such as porches, trellising and fencing can all help to reduce wind speeds without increasing heat loss from the building. Vegetation, carefully planned, can act as a "third skin" on appropriate walls of buildings by providing wind drag and an additional thermal buffer. In effect it becomes "free" and renewable insulation material with minimal manufacturing costs[8] (Figure 3.15).

Housing layouts should be self-sheltering wherever possible. The traditional Scottish village (Figure 3.16) provides a good rural example of this with the tight layout of buildings creating a milder micro-climate and helping to shelter the inner faces and entrances of the buildings. The traditional Victorian tenement block provides an urban example of the same principle.

The use of trees combined with planting and fencing in garden areas also provides some degree of **wind shelter through landcover.** The most effective height for trees is the height of the dwelling and placed 1-3 heights away, or 3-4 heights where solar access is required[9] (Figure 3.17). Larger shelterbelts of trees can provide the same effect over a whole housing development. There may be a conflict with the need for visibility and observation when providing planting. This can be overcome by planning lines of vision along public routes from the housing.

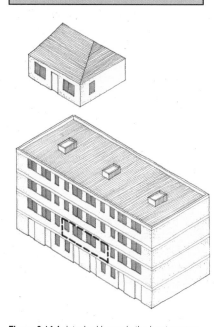

Figure 3.14 A detached house is the least energy efficient form in that heat loss can occur from all sides. For the same floor area a property within a tenement block is protected on at least one side and often top and bottom by surrounding properties minimising heat loss through the fabric of the building.

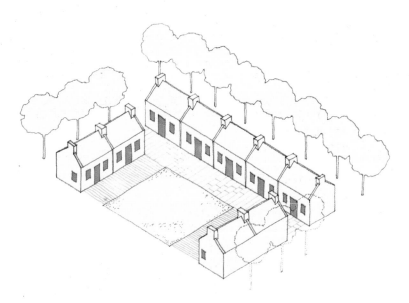

Figure 3.16 Layout of traditional Scottish village to shelter from harsh elements and take full advantage of sun.

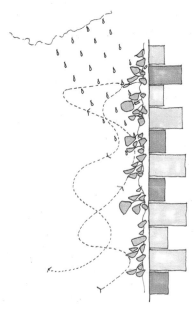

Figure 3.15 Vegetation, as third skin, on a building can offer protection from the elements and reduce pollution.

---

[8] Johnston and Newton (1993)
[9] BRECSU (1995b) p7

Figure 3.17 Shelter belts of trees should be planted at a distance of 1 to 3 x house height from the building to maximise wind drag. In addition fences in front of the building can assist this further (After Borer and Harris 1998).

Box 3.3	Reducing wind chill and heat loss: pointers for good practice

- avoid exposed, windy sites and take advantage of any shelter offered by a site
- visit site to establish local wind conditions and design for these
- orientate housing to minimise wind chill by presenting narrow ends to the prevailing wind
- minimise surface to volume area of buildings by maximising use of terrace or tenement layouts and using compact forms
- use shared party walls to reduce heat loss through the building envelope
- increase shelter and wind drag through use of planting and external structures
- design housing to be self-sheltering
- avoid housing layouts and forms that accelerate the wind
- use evergreen planting to increase effectiveness of shelterbelts in winter but avoid overshading

3.1.3 Precipitation: Design For The Effects Of Climate Change

Housing developments should be "future proofed" against increased precipitation and storm frequency[10] with suitably robust layout and detailing. Consultants should be asked if they have taken the predicted effects of global climate change, such as increased storms and precipitation, into account[11] (see Box 3.4).

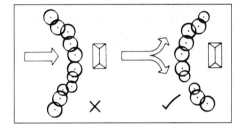

Figure 3.18A. A correctly curved shelter belt will help to deflect wind, depending on tree type, density, height, etc.

---

[10] Climatic Research Unit (1998)
[11] BRE Scottish Laboratory (1998)

Box 3.4   **Taking account of global climate change:
pointers for good practice**

- check existing water table and natural patterns of drainage
- calculate rainwater guttering and pipework on the basis of up to 30% increase in precipitation
- use soft landscaping to reduce storm water runoff and help the rain to percolate naturally back into the water table[12] (Figure 3.19)
- use porous paving schemes to allow water to flow down through hard landscaping directly into the water table to minimise drainage requirements and relieve pressure on existing drainage (Figure 3.20)
- retain robust roofing details including sarking in preference to battens
- ensure all details take account of increased intensity and number of storms
- preserve and increase planting of trees to absorb CO_2 to help reduce global climate change

Figure 3.19 Swale Drain. Soft landscaping allows surface water to drain away naturally

3.1.4 Temperature: Using Landcover To Modify Extremes

Large urban areas in Scotland create particular local climates which trap pollution, have less solar radiation, and are generally warmer than the surrounding countryside by several degrees. Planting modifies heat difference by trapping solar heat and providing cool air through transpiration. Hard landscaping in the immediate vicinity of the dwelling can also capture solar heat during the day and re-radiate it in the evening which helps to even out daily temperature swings (see Case Study No.5).

To replenish the oxygen we use up, each human needs 30 m² of planting, either in housing schemes or elsewhere. Trees are effectively the "lungs" of the Earth. They not only clean air by removing 75% of dust particles, they oxygenate it, and remove carbon dioxide as well as sulphur monoxide[13]. Meanwhile their roots break down the soil, take up nutrients and provide the soil with nutrients in return through dead leaf mould. Scotland's major cities have some of the highest concentrations of air pollutants in Europe, principally arising from traffic. In inner city areas the use of trees and other planting can act as a pollution filter between housing and busy, congested roads.

Figure 3.20 The use of porous paving and blocks can help rainwater drain away naturally saving significantly on underground pipework.

---

[12] SEPA (1998)
[13] Giradet (1992)

Trees are also of high amenity value and can form a focus for community involvement by combining community woodland development with housing[14]. Many of our housing estates have few trees because landscaping is traditionally the first cost saving to be made. This is shortsighted given the environmental benefits that trees and planting in generally can generate.

Box 3.5	Soft and hard landscaping : pointers for good practice

- require contractors to preserve biodiversity
- minimise hard landscaping and encourage the use of deciduous trees to enhance microclimate
- preserve existing mature trees and wildflower areas as much as possible
- increase planting generally to increase opportunities for local wildlife to proliferate
- set aside wild areas using native plants and trees with minimal cultivation to encourage local biodiversity
- provide corridors of linked planting to allow cross-pollination and provide routes for wildlife
- establish which parts of the site are optimum for growing vegetation and allow re-development to take place on the least ecologically promising part of the site
- replace soil sterilised by additional housing with soil and plant cover on the roofs of the housing (Figure 3.21) where suitable
- use planting as pollution filters and sound barriers between busy, congested roads and housing developments
- use hard landscaping on south side of building as thermal mass to modify climate

3.2

Site Contamination

The increasing use of brownfield sites often means dealing with contaminated sites. Consultants should establish an accurate site history using local records and carry out a contamination survey where necessary.

Site de-contamination can be carried out in a number of ways:

- scrape clean and removal of toxic soil
- capping the contaminated soil
- chemical de-contamination
- biological de-contamination

The most benign method involving least energy is biological de-contamination using toxin-neutralising plants such as willow saplings and reeds(Figures 3.22 - 3.23).

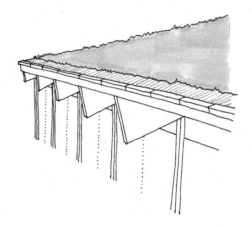

Figure 3.21 Soil and plant cover on roofs replace planting sterilized on the ground by new buildings.

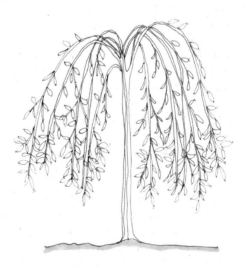

Figure 3.22 - 2.23 Planting of willows and reeds can naturally assist with de-contamination of site.

[14] The CD-ROM *Quality Green Space for Residential Areas* produced by Scottish Homes, COSLA, Scottish House Builders Association and Scottish Natural Heritage (1999) provides practical guidance and best practice on community greenspace by working with local communities. The CD-ROM is freely available from SNH with supporting documentation.

This takes time, however, and requires careful pre-planning. Intensive treatment for on site de-contamination using enhanced chemical compositions can be quicker but uses a more energy intensive product. Capping the contamination does not get rid of the problem but may be a cost effective solution if contamination is not severe. Scraping the site clean is a last resort but may be required if contamination is particularly severe. Consultants should balance the cost of de-contamination process against the environmental impact of the de-contamination process itself.[15]

3.3

A Sense Of Place

The final ingredient when designing sustainably for a given site is to understand the existing nature of the locality. Physical, historical, cultural and archeological features all inform a sense of place and should also be taken into consideration when applying **a holistic approach** to site development. Sustainable design is as much about sustaining our history as it is about sustaining our environment.

Site Checklist-Key Areas

Climate
- carry out comprehensive climate analysis
- maximise passive solar gain (see Box 3.2)
- provide shelter by modifying housing layout and form (see Box 3.3)
- take account of global climate change (see Box 3.4)

Land cover
- protect and enhance existing vegetation (see Box 3.5)
- make provision for contaminated site remediation

Sense of place
- note historical, cultural or archeological features on the site
- identify physical influences on local building style

---

[15] For comparison of treatments for contaminated land see CIRIA (1995 onwards) also CIRIA (1991)

Chapter Four
Energy Use

Housing providers have a role to play in helping local authorities to meet the energy targets set out in the Home Energy Conservation Act of 1995 by auditing their stock and establishing strategies to meet them. In the long term, the experience that RSLs gain in this area can be used to help all home owners and housing providers address energy efficiency.

Scottish Homes Sustainable Development Policy[1] also lays down specific energy targets to be met by all housing funded by them. The targets are easily achievable and should be taken as a *minimum* standard. In many instances it may be possible to increase the SAP rating level to nearer 100 using optimum design strategies.

Scottish Homes Sustainable Development Policy Energy Targets

New build SAP rating no less than 85-90
Rehabilitation SAP rating no less than 65-70

This Chapter outlines the basic principles for reducing energy use and offers guidance on the following:

- energy surveying
- the basics of energy efficient design
- energy conservation in the building envelope
- daylighting and artificial lighting
- preventing heat loss through ventilation
- renewable energy
- energy efficient delivery systems
- energy efficient systems in the dwelling

---

[1] Scottish Homes (1999c)

4.1

Energy Surveying

The basis of any strategic approach to saving energy must start with a careful survey of existing stock. Once this has been carried out a programme can be drawn up which targets housing in need of upgrading on a systematic basis[2]. Apart from helping to form an energy strategy, energy surveys can give the following benefits:

- tailored energy advice to occupiers[3]
- identify energy grant eligibility for occupiers[4]
- inform maintenance strategy and life cycle costing
- provides base line for future energy auditing.

There are a number of different energy and environmental rating schemes available which are usually carried out by qualified assessors. The four most well known are:

- SAP (Standard Assessment Procedure)
- NHER (National Home Energy Rating Scheme)
- BREEAM (Building Research Establishment Environmental Assessment Method)
- BRE Environmental Standard Award

The SAP[5] is a requirement under Building Regulations for all new build dwellings to ensure they are energy efficient. It has a rating from 1-100, the higher the better. It is a relatively crude assessment of annual energy costs which takes no account of local climate, occupancy patterns, or heating patterns. The rating is based on fuel cost rather than CO_2 emissions which can lead to distortions. It is also sensitive to boiler controls, favouring condensing boilers under any circumstance, even when they might not be required.

The NHER[6] system operates at a variety of levels of sophistication and is more sensitive than SAP, taking into account local climate and location details. It operates on a scale of 1-10, again the higher the better. In addition NHER can also take account of occupant behaviour and the condition of the dwelling when used at a higher level. It is generally slightly more expensive to carry out than the SAP but yields more meaningful results.

The Environmental Standard[7] is the current Version 3 of BREEAM (the Building Research Establishment Environmental Assessment Method) and it concerns new homes. This gives credits for a variety of environmental measures adopted, including energy efficiency, and offers a broader rating than either SAP or NHER.

---

[2] BRECSU(SAVE)

[3] BRECSU (1996) gives useful guidance on providing energy advice to householders

[4] These may be available from the local authority or under government programmes through the Energy Savings Trust

[5] SAP is available as a worksheet from HMSO or as part of the building regulations Part L, 1995 edition, also from HMSO. More information is available from BRE.

[6] Information on NHER is available from the National Energy Foundation (NEF) on their website http:\\www.natenergy.org.uk

[7] Available from BRE

It can be used to examine the overall environmental impact of housing stock. There is also an additional cost to receive the accreditation. It is currently being updated and will be launched as the new Environmental Standard for Homes.

4.2

The Basics Of Energy Efficient Design

Energy efficiency is an integrated approach to insulation, ventilation, solar gain, daylighting, thermal mass, heating and control systems. It is important always to consider these aspects in relation to each other.

Space heating counteracting heat loss through the external building fabric is the primary form of energy consumption in Scottish housing. **The optimum use of energy is to get a balanced system which uses as much free heat gain as possible to offset minimised heat losses and energy consumption.**

> **sources of free heat gain in dwellings**
> - sunlight
> - occupants (80 watts each)
> - cooking heat
> - hot water usage
> - waste heat from lights
> - waste heat from domestic appliances

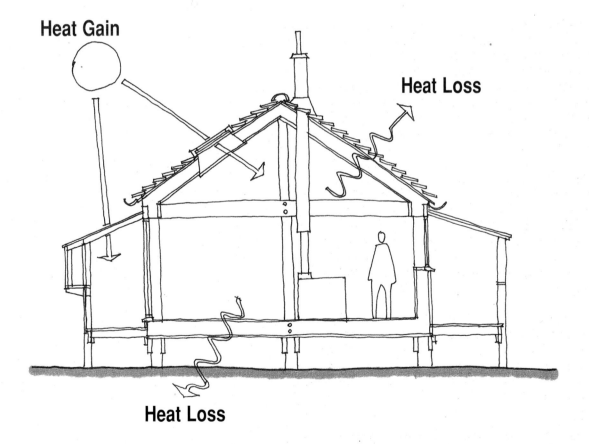

Figure 4.3 Heat gains should be maximised and heat loss minimised (After Borer and Harris, 1998).

4.2.1 Energy conservation in the building envelope

Reducing energy demand in housing is the first priority, followed by the use of renewable energy sources for heating wherever possible. **The retrofitting of proper levels of insulation to existing housing stock is the single most cost effective way to save energy and cut down on global climate change emissions from the housing sector in Scotland** (see Section 8.1.3). Other benefits of retrofitting insulation are:

* financial payback to the housing provider through reduced service requirements
* preservation of building fabric
* condensation-free dwelling
* healthy and warm dwelling for the occupier
* low fuel bills
* increased air tightness and control of ventilation.

The following levels of insulation are appropriate for the UK, depending on the type of construction:[9]

roof	300-450 mm
wall	150-300 mm
floor	150-250mm

These levels of insulation are not always achievable in retrofit schemes but the great majority of existing dwellings can be improved to at least 1990 Building Regulation levels within reasonable costs[10].

It is preferable to use an organic, natural material for insulation where this is possible to minimise environmental and health impacts (see Table 4.2). Insulation materials are generally lightweight and bulky therefore long distance transportation should be avoided if possible.

Housing providers should assess their stock on the basis of individual dwelling type and orientation where possible (see Table 4.1)[11] and decide which form of insulation is most appropriate for them on balance. Effective guidance on the cost-benefits of retro-fitting different insulation systems in Scotland is available from the Scottish Executive as well as others.[12]

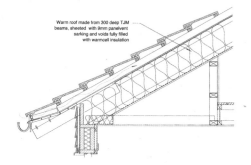

Figure 4.4 A typical roof detail for a highly insulated house.

© John Gilbert

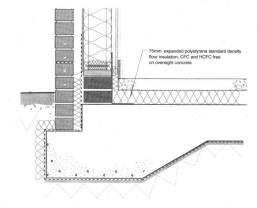

Figure 4.5 A typical wall and floor detail for a highly insulated house, which avoids cold penetrating at the junction between the wall and floor.

© John Gilbert

[9] See Borer and Harris (1998) p.151 for more detail
[10] Bell and Lowe (1995)
[11] It is not always economic to assess each dwelling individually, but doing so ensures that insulation retrofitting strategies are accurate and allows for all variations
[12] Scottish Office Building Directorate (1995), BRE (1990b)

Table 4.1	Factors affecting choice of insulation strategy	
Key factors	external insulation	internal insulation
ease of installation	requires scaffolding exposed to weather affects access to building	awkward detailing confined space occupants need to be decanted
type of construction	fixing system to suit construction preparation of external surfaces required	cavity fill best where possible in walling dry-lining detailing depends whether construction is solid or not
type of heating regime requirements	suitable for constant slow response heating requirement with thermal mass	suitable for intermittent fast response heating requirement with no thermal mass
type of insulant	rigid boarding required complex systems: rainscreen cladding using sheet panels polymer render on mesh base difficult to use natural insulants	drylining walls suits natural insulants relatively simple system care required with solid flooring and sloping roofs
energy payback	relatively slow with complex systems varies between 5-30 years depending on detailing and materials used	relatively fast cavity fill and loft I year wall drylining 5 years
aesthetics	very effective for altering profile and exterior of building not always suitable for conservation areas or listed buildings	no effect on exterior of building can present awkward detailing internally to avoid cold bridging
financial payback	relatively slow varies between 17-55 years	relatively fast especially for cavity fill and loft 2-3 years
life cycle impact and health	tends to have high embodied energy with high environmental impact minimal health impacts for occupants	low embodied energy especially when using natural insulants care needs to be taken with certain foam insulants that off-gas into the dwelling
maintenance	requires re-painting for smooth render systems, otherwise as for external cladding	no additional maintenance beyond internal finishes. Loose fill fibres in walls may settle after a year and require topping up.

Table 4.2
Types of Insulation available[13] for different dwelling elements

Material	Roof options	Wall options	Floor options
Organic Natural Renewable Reuseable Low embodied energy	*loft:* cellulose flax hemp sheeps wool wood wool wood fibre *flat roof:* cork	*internal insulation or timber frame:* cellulose cork flax hemp sheeps wool wood wool wood fibre *cavity fill:* none recommended	*suspended:* as for loft *solid:* as for flat roof
Inorganic Minerals Non-renewable Reuseable High embodied energy	*loft:* rockwool, fibreglass perlite vermiculite *flat roof:* foamed glass rockwool fibreglass	*internal insulation or timber frame:* rockwool, fibreglass *cavity fill:* foamed glass rockwool fibreglass	*suspended:* rockwool, fibreglass *solid:* rockwool, fibreglass perlite vermiculite
Fossil Organic Oil-derivatives Difficult to re-use High embodied energy Off-gassing present	*loft:* expanded polystyrene extruded polystyrene polyisocyanurate foam polyurethane foam urea and phenol formaldehyde foam *flat roof:* expanded polystyrene extruded polystyrene polyisocyanurate foam polyurethane foam urea and phenol formaldehyde foam	*internal insulation or timber frame:* expanded polystyrene extruded polystyrene poly-isocyanurate foam polyurethane foam urea and phenol formaldehyde foam *cavity fill:* expanded polystyrene extruded polystyrene polyisocyanurate foam polyurethane foam urea and phenol formaldehyde foam	*suspended:* expanded polystyrene extruded polystyrene polyisocyanurate foam polyurethane foam urea and phenol formaldehyde foam *solid:* expanded polystyrene extruded polystyrene polyisocyanurate foam polyurethane foam urea and phenol formaldehyde foam

Figure 4.6 Cellulose insulation used as internal insulation has low embodied energy and is recycled.

Figure 4.7 Natural raw wool can be used for insulation. It is also available in rollbatts from manufacturers.

Figure 4.8 Unfired earth blocks can be used in housing, saving significant embodied energy compared to fired bricks.

[13] see Borer and Harris (1998) p.100-104 for more detail on different natural insulants

Windows can account for up to 10% heat loss in a well insulated dwelling and should be specified with as much insulation as the housing provider can afford. Double glazing with low emissivity films and inert gas is now standard practice in many cases but this can be significantly improved on by the use of double casement windows. These have one frame with double glazing coupled to one with single glazing. The increased frame depth and air gap between the two glazing units can double the insulation value.

Box 4.1	Insulation strategy : pointers for good practice

- maximise insulation to roof, wall and floor
- use breathing, natural and low energy insulation products where possible
- combine adopted heating strategy with appropriate insulation system
- a little insulation retrofitted is better than none at all
- use windows with U-value range 0.6-1.2 using double glazing frame coupled to single glazed frame where possible

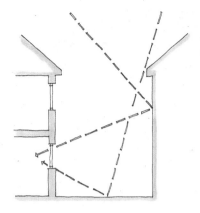

Figure 4.9 Reflectance can add significantly to daylighting levels indoors.

4.2.2 Daylighting and artificial lighting

Minimising energy used in lighting becomes a key issue once housing is more energy efficient than current building regulations. The aim should be to maximise daylighting while minimising artificial lighting (see Box 4.2)[14]. Glazing generally loses about six times as much energy as a well insulated wall or roof and a balance must be struck between providing daylighting and minimising heat losses.

Daylight is dependent on the amount of open sky available outside a window, the amount of sunshine available and the amount of reflectance of light from surrounding surfaces. The size, angle and shape of openings together with room height depth and decoration determine the distribution of the daylight (Figures 4.9 - 4.11).

Sun angles range from 10 degrees from the horizontal in the winter in the far north of Scotland to 60 degrees in the summer further south. Windows should be carefully designed to maximise sunlight penetration into rooms without glare. (see Figure 4.12) Given the low sun angles that mark the Scottish winter, glare can be a particular problem caused by strong contrast between light from a window and its surround.

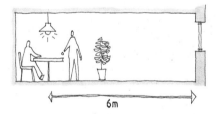

Figure 4.10 Generally, daylight will not be adequate beyond 4-6m from the window for housing.

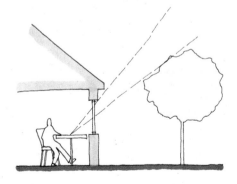

Figure 4.11 Daylight is dependent on the amount of open sky available.

---

[14] see BRE (1993, 1994) for energy efficient artificial lighting.

daylighting:

- check site for daylight obstructions and position building form to overcome these
- design form and layout of dwelling to maximise daylight penetration
- design glazing and openings to optimise daylight in rooms

avoid glare by:

- external planting regimes and filtering devices
- light colouring of internal decoration especially window frames and surrounds
- splayed window reveals (Figure 4.12)
- internal shading devices such as venetian blinds
- introducing light from more than one direction
- indirect lighting by reflectance from light surfaces
- external self-shading offered by building form

artificial lighting:

- use low-energy light bulbs (can save up to 40 per cent on electricity bills in a well insulated house)[15]
- use efficient lighting and specify high frequency control gear for flourescents
- avoid internal rooms and stores which require artificial light
- ensure all common areas are naturally daylit
- use light colours on walls, floors and ceilings to increase efficiency of lighting

Figure 4.12 Splayed windows reveals are a traditional Scottish feature and help prevent glare.

4.2.3 Preventing heat loss through ventilation

Ventilation can account for up to 25 per cent of heat loss in a typical house. Conventional housing has 3-5 air changes an hour which has to be warmed in winter. Effective detailing against air leakage and draughtproofing[16] can reduce this to 0.5 -1 air changes an hour. Timber frame construction is easier to make airtight than masonry, and loose fill insulation, such as cellulose, can help fill in gaps between construction elements.

Mechanical heat recovery systems recover heat lost through ventilation by extracting heat from exhaust air and using it to pre-heat incoming fresh air[17]. They range in size from small air brick size units (Figure 4.13) to large systems housed in the

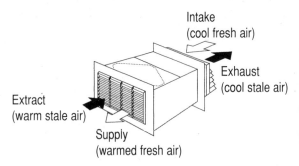

Figure 4.13 Heat recovery fan units can be small and unobtrusive in kitchens and bathrooms.

---

[15] see BRE (1994)
[16] BRE (1986) BRECSU (1995a)
[17] BRE(1994a)

loft. The small units can be effective where mechanical extraction is required by regulation. The larger systems tend to involve substantial ductwork, are difficult to retrofit and can be noisy. They are not recommended for use in dwellings with over 1 air change an hour as efficiency is lost.

Passive stack ventilation allows exhaust air to rise up through the dwelling naturally using extract pipes that exit at the ridge of the roof. Its main advantage is that it uses no mechanical energy, has no moving parts and can replace mechanical ventilation for building regulation purposes[18]. It requires adequate height to create a steady flow. There are now a number of proprietary systems available which compare favourably to mechanical extract systems (Figure 4.14)

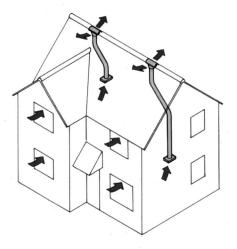

Figure 4.14 A simple passive stack ventilation system replaces the need for energy hungry extract fans.

Box 4.3	Preventing heat loss through ventilation: pointers for good practice

- ensure adequate draughtproofing to all windows and doors
- use timber frame construction for better air-tightness
- pay attention to all jointing details and seal them
- use loose blown fibre insulation rather than rolls or batts
- use small heat recovery units where mechanical ventilation is required
- use passive ventilation systems where possible

4.3

Renewable Energy

Renewable energy is any source of energy that effectively replenishes itself and is inexhaustible. Currently most energy for housing comes from finite and unsustainable fuel sources such as natural gas, coal and nuclear power. Housing providers should aim to incorporate renewable energy into their new developments and existing housing stock wherever possible[19]. The use of renewable energy has the following benefits:

- minimises the use of non-renewable fossil fuels
- minimises air pollution
- a "clean" source of energy
- a "free" source of energy to the user

Renewable energy systems should not be used as a primary means of addressing energy efficiency. They come into their own once initial conservation measures have been taken and only a relatively small amount of water heating or electricity is required (see Case Study No.3). **It is always more cost effective to conserve energy than to produce it in housing.** Solar power is the easiest to use in urban situations, while rural sites can benefit from the other forms of renewable energy such as wind or water.

---

[18] see BRE(1994b)
[19] A good general introduction to renewable energy is Boyle (1996)

Table 4.3   **Renewable Energy options**

Key factors	active solar[20]	wind[21]	hydro[22]	biomass[23]
type of installation	photovoltaic (PV) panels for electricity or water/evacuated air panels for heating/hot water	windturbines providing electricity from small diameter 50w to large commercial turbines providing 0.5mw or more	ranges from small micro-hydro turbine running off constant stream with a drop to large commercial dams and river installations	straw, wood or various fast growing crops can be harvested for burning to create energy.
ease of installation	can be installed as part of roof (new build) or retrofitted re-plumbing required for existing water tank only appropriate for south facing roofs with minimum pitch of 30^0	depends on size larger installations require large foundations and should be sited at a distance from any dwellings	easiest with small stream and high head of water requires pipework and concretework to house turbine	requires large amount of land sited near to fuel burning facility. 300-500m^2 of coppice for space heating one dwelling
heating regime requirements	solar panels most effective in summer (up to 80% of hot water supply). best for hot water only rather than space heating. PVs not effective for heating.	provides renewable energy for electrical heating –most effective in winter. heating demand should be relatively constant as there is an energy storage limitation	provides renewable energy for electrical heating –most effective in winter. energy storage limitations. more reliable than either wind or sun.	best with low constant heating. effective all year round but requires storage space (5m^3 per dwelling per year for wood)
embodied energy payback	7-12 years	0.5 years	N/a	minimal
aesthetics	problems of integrating panels on existing stock in urban/conservation areas	needs careful siting in rural areas. does not affect dwelling	pipework should be underground ideally turbine house and dams need integration with landscape	monocultural cropping can look unsightly and out of place as well as restricting views
financial payback	10 –15 years for water panels photovoltaics do not payback over their lifetime yet	depends on size – larger installations pay back more quickly 7.5 >12.5 years	small scale systems can pay back within 7 – 8 years	8-10 years depending on size of scheme and species planted
life cycle impact and health	minimal health impacts-clean technology. some environmental impact from products	beating noise can be intrusive if sited to close to housing- otherwise clean technology some environmental impacts from turbines	minimal health impacts –clean technology micro-hydro has minimal environmental impact larger schemes have more impact	fuel must be burnt cleanly to avoid toxic emissions possible impact on biodiversity
maintenance	life expectancy of panels 15-20 years servicing required	life expectancy of turbines can be 20 years or more servicing required	very long life expectancy turbines can run for 30-60 years	minimal maintenance requires intensive input for harvesting and maintenance of crops

[20] British Standards Institution(1990) gives standard guidance on solar panel systems.
Centre For Alternative Technology(1997)
Borer and Harris (1998) p225-235 gives a good description of active solar systems.
Centre for Alternative Technology Components of Renewable Energy Systems Resource Guide
[21] Piggott (1995) gives a simple guide to small scale wind power, Smerdon (1997) for autonomous energy systems
[22] Curtis (1999), Smerdon (1997)
Centre for Alternative Technology Water Power Resource Guide, Smerdon (1997)
[23] Macpherson (1995) Introduces Bio-mass cropping, Smerdon (1997) for autonomous cropping.

4.4.

Energy Efficient Delivery Systems

An understanding of how energy is delivered to a housing development allows the housing provider to take advantage of the most efficient delivery system for a particular site. The provider often has little control over the primary means of how energy is supplied to a site and most existing Scottish housing stock still relies either on gas, or electric heating from non-renewable fossil fuel resources.

Electric heating systems should be avoided because they generally produce between two to four times the overall amount of CO_2 emissions compared to gas central heating when the full production cycle is taken into account. If electric systems are to be fitted on grounds of availability, capital costs and maintenance, their efficiency should be optimised through the use of renewable energy or combined heat and power schemes where possible.

4.4.1 Communal Heating, District Heating and CHP (combined heat and power)

It is inefficient to install normal size boilers and central heating systems for well insulated individual dwellings. A common heat source can greatly reduce the number of boilers required and subsequent maintenance. The advantage of this form of supply is that it is highly flexible in terms of fuel source; renewable energy, waste heat, gas or electricity can all be used[24]. Communal heating provides heating for one housing scheme whereas district heating supplies a whole area.

Combined Heat and Power generation (CHP) goes one step further than communal and district heating by maximising the efficiency of the production of electricity. The waste heat produced by an electricity generator is used to provide hot water for heating. The generator can be as small as a van engine (see Case Study No.12 and Figure 4.15) but CHP works best on a district basis, where there is a constant demand for both heating and electricity. Perthshire Housing Association is currently investigating a CHP scheme which will link up a hospital, school and housing; the different providers requiring heating at different times maximises the efficiency of the system.

Both communal heating and CHP schemes present issues in relation to fuel charging. Housing providers can choose between a flat rate charge or individual metering. The former can be wasteful and unfair on individual tenants, while the latter may be expensive to install and manage. Different housing associations have overcome these issues in different ways (see Case Study Nos. 3, 4 and 12 and Table 4.4).

---

[24] see Lowe (1996) p.123-132 for a full discussion on district heating and CHP

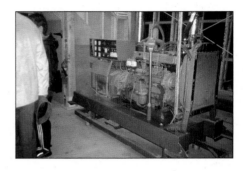

Figure 4.15 This CHP engine is large enough to power a small housing scheme.

Table 4.4   Options for Energy Efficient Delivery Systems

Key factors	individual dwelling heating	communal heating	district heating[25]	combined heat and power[26]
type of installation	central heating or point heating delivered by gas or electricity	single heating source can serve single housing development	single heating source can serve large area of town or city	single heating source can serve communal or district scheme uses waste heat from electricity generator to supply hot water for heating
installation requirements	re-wiring for electrical systems and re-plumbing for gas systems, individual point source heaters or radiators and a boiler	compact housing layout simple and accessible external pipe runs central plant room required	as for communal heating, pipe runs should run under public pavements	can be small combustion engine for communal heating[27] or power station for district heating
heating regime requirements	convectors and radiators can be used for intermittent or fast response heating storage heaters are for slow response heating individually metered on fuel used	operates best with low temperature radiators	operates best with low temperature radiators	requires constant demand for heat and electricity for efficiency operates best with low temperature radiators
metering	individually metered and billed	can be individually metered (expensive) or charged on flat rate or mix of both (best)	as with communal heating most efficient option is to offer flat rate with individual top up supplied by individual electricity supply	as for communal and district heating with electricity metered (expensive) or operated on pre-payment card[28]
financial arrangements	installation paid and serviced by housing provider or owner occupier	installation paid and serviced by housing provider with service charge	as for communal heating or using 3rd party to install and service (partnership with energy supplier)	as for district heating requires partnership with others who might use heat and electricity on a more constant basis (hospital, sheltered housing etc)
maintenance requirements	maintenance of individual heating systems by housing provider. High for gas central heating, low for electric	maintenance of distribution network and central plant by housing provider with option of 3rd party maintenance contract	as for communal heating negotiation required with other authorities where pipework extends beyond site	as for district heating

---

[25] BRECSU (1994a)
[26] Combined Heat and Power Association (1995)
[27] ETSU GPG1
[28] BRECSU (1998)

4.4.2 Geothermal Energy

There is a particular opportunity for housing in the Central Belt area of Scotland where many old mine workings have relatively warm water sitting in them. The low-grade heat that exists deep under the surface of the Earth can be upgraded using heat pumps within a housing scheme situated on top of the mineworkings or immediately adjacent. There can be considerable savings on fossil fuels as the heat may be of the order of 13°C all year round, requiring a top-up heat input of only a few degrees to provide adequate central heating (see Case Study No. 3).

4.5

Energy Efficient Systems In The Dwelling

Once the sources of energy supply have been decided it becomes important to optimise elements within the dwelling for energy efficiency. A key component is the accurate sizing of heating systems. Many housing schemes fail to achieve energy targets because of the mismatch between high insulation levels and heating specifications. With high insulation, condensing boilers may not be necessary (Figures 4.16 - 4.17). In many instances, point sources of heating rather than the standard package of central heating, will be adequate and save on energy use, maintenance, cost and resource use in manufacture. There are now a number of smaller heating installations available for the low energy dwelling[29].

The lower the operating temperature of a heating system the wider the range of energy sources it can use giving the greatest upgradeability and flexibility. For this reason low temperature radiator systems or underfloor heating are preferable to high temperature radiator systems

Figure 4.16 Convential oversized condensing boiler.

Figure 4.17 Correctly sized smaller boiler for hot water only.

---

[29] see Hall and Warm (1998) for listings in UK

variables	individual gas central heating	individual point sources/electric heating	renewable energy systems
delivery mode	condensing boiler direct or indirect hot water system	electric heaters gas wall heaters	solar water panels linked into indirect system photoelectric panels (PV) feeding electrical mains
sizing	avoid oversizing of boilers and radiators may be unnecessary altogether	can be used for very small heating loads	solar hot water = 4m² per dwelling photoelectric panels = 80 -100 watts each (600x1200mm panel)
controls	avoid overcomplex programmes ensure that condensing boilers can operate in condensing mode (low temperature)	controls tend to be very basic (thermostat but no timer) - may not be responsive to occupancy patterns	needs sophisticated programmer to balance solar gains against standard form of heating (occupiers need training in use)
flexibility	boiler position determined by layout	electric heaters are highly flexible gas heaters need positioning on an outside wall	panels only suitable for certain roofs (correct orientation and pitch)
upgrading	system may need downsizing replacement of boiler	simple replacement of point heaters	panels should be replaceable as efficiency increases

Table 4.5   Energy efficient systems in dwelling

Energy Checklist-Key Areas

Form and fabric

- carry out energy audit on existing stock and adopt an achievable insulation programme (see Section 4.1)
- incorporate optimum levels of insulation to all fabric elements before anything else (see Box 4.1)
- design building envelope to ensure air tightness and avoid cold bridging (see Box 4.3)
- optimise daylighting (see Box 4.2)

Systems

- select appropriate delivery system for heating (see Table 4.4)
- specify high energy efficiency space and water heating systems - avoid oversizing
- realise full potential of renewable energy sources (see Table 4.3)
- incorporate effective and easily understood control systems
- ensure integration between the energy system proposed and other aspects of human comfort
- use natural ventilation or passive stack ventilation in preference to mechanical ventilation (see Section 4.2.3)
- specify gas heating in preference to electric heating where possible
- use low temperature radiators to allow for a variety of low temperature energy sources.
- check energy efficiency measures repay their embodied energy over the product lifetime (see Table 4.3)

Chapter Five
Resource Conservation

A major aim of sustainable housing must be to exploit all viable opportunities to recycle and reuse products and buildings in order to reduce production in the first place. **It cannot be stressed too strongly how important it is to look at each housing development's potential for efficient and responsible resource use within its own unique and local context** (Figure 5.1).

This Chapter offers guidance on the following key areas for resource conservation:

* local sourcing
* waste minimisation
* embodied energy and environmental impact
* lifecycles of buildings, products and materials.

5.1

Local Sourcing

Specifying products and materials which are sourced and/or manufactured in the locality of a housing development brings the following benefits (see Case Study No. 2):

* less environmental impact in terms of transportation
* direct relationship between housing providers and the local economy
* easy visiting and monitoring by specifiers who wish to verify the sustainability of products
* local employment linked to the housing development
* increased sense of community through local connections.

It is not always possible to obtain local products and materials which provide the same quality and performance as imported products for a similar cost. Where local sourcing is possible, care must be taken not to contravene free-trade agreements within the European Union. Specifiers should ask for products in terms of a performance specification. It is then possible to write in "local availability" and "minimum transportation" clauses (with a stated distance) as one of the performance requirements. An alternative to this would be to write the performance requirement to match the exact specification of the local product, paying attention to any unique features it may have.

Figure 5.1 Traditional Scottish housing uses local materials and detailing to suit the local climate.

Figure 5.2 Long distance transportation of construction materials has a detrimental impact on the environment and people's health through pollution and noise.

47

Box 5.1   Local sourcing: pointers for good practice

- ask contractors and consultants to source materials and products which are available locally and find out how they intend to do so

- weigh up the use of local resources against their potential environmental impact both globally and locally

- use performance specifications with clauses which favour local sourcing

- source raw and bulk materials as locally as possible to minimise transportation

Figure 5.3 If stone cannot be recycled it is best to source new materials as locally as possible.

Figure 5.4 Re-used stone minimises our use of non-renewable resources and should be specified when available.

Table 5.1　　Sourcing local information

Environmental Factor	Site Level Sourcing	Local Sourcing Information	Global Impact Information
1. Raw materials consumption	sustainable use of natural resources on site	local manufacturers Yellow pages local trade organisations	manufacturing associations environmental groups such as Friends of the Earth reports government reports and websites
2. Biodiversity/Flora and Fauna	Site audit Website for Scottish indigenous flora http://fff.nhm.ac.uk/fff/	Scottish Natural Heritage - Local Office	manufacturer product information - effect on global scale reports by environmental groups such as World Wildlife Fund, Scottish Wildlife Trust Scottish Natural Heritage - main Office in Edinburgh
3. Toxic emissions to air,water and earth	site audit for ground, air and water contamination; historical maps, previous site records	SEPA environmental health departments	manufacturer product information LCA systems for product impact
4. Water consumption	site audit of natural resources water authorities	SEPA Water authorities meterological Office for rainfall details	manufacturer information environmental groups
5. Energy use	site audit of available renewable resources: sun, wind, water, biomass, geo-thermal	local energy companies local audit of waste heat resources for CHP/district heating identify energy partnerships	embodied energy - manufacturers product information and independent audits
6. Solid waste	site audit for re-use/recycling of waste matter re-use/recycling of existing building materials	other local reusable/recyclable material available? salvage yards SEPA Local Authority	manufacturer product information LCA systems for product impact environmental group reports
7. Health impacts	site audit for health impacts: noise pollution, electromagnetic radiation etc.	Local audit for potential health impacts environmental health department Health Authorities	manufacturers product information and independent audits by environmental groups
8. Economic impacts	audit of surrounding area around site for local manufacturing of construction products	local enterprise companies to identify local construction manufacturing companies establish partnerships with local authorities	manufacturers information on global economics environmental group reports on products
9. Social impacts	consult users adjacent to site and on site	consult local community groups Local Plans	manufacturers product information on social impacts

5.2

Waste Minimisation And Pollution

The five main areas of waste to address are:

- construction waste
- prefabrication
- re-use and recycling
- water conservation
- domestic waste.

5.2.1 Construction waste

Prevention of waste in the construction of housing can save considerable amounts of non-renewable resources. Housing providers can encourage good site practice by requiring waste minimisation strategies to be provided and used during the construction process by the contractor (see Case Study No.2). These should be referred to in housing design guides and requested in contract documentation[1].

5.2.2 Prefabrication to minimise waste

The Egan Report[2] has set targets for reducing defects by 20% and costs by 10% in the construction industry and has suggested that prefabrication can go a long way to achieving this. The main advantages of prefabrication are:

- factory controlled conditions for manufacture minimising the effect of weather
- standardised units with minimum offcuts
- quick assembly with greater precision
- just in time delivery requiring minimum site storage
- minimised defects.

Prefabrication in housing can take the form of timber, steel and concrete units which incorporate fully finished secondary elements such as glazing, services and finishes. The units can vary from simple non-loadbearing cassettes (Figure 5.6) that form walling, flooring or roofing, to comprehensive load-bearing systems that come as a complete package. There are a number of proprietary systems on the market which housing providers can specify (see Case Study No.6)[3]. Ideally, prefabrication should occur as locally as possible to minimise the impact of transportation and link local knowledge with the

Figure 5.5 Contractors should be required to implement waste minimisation strategies to prevent this.

Figure 5.6 Prefabrication gives factory controlled precision on site.

---

[1] CIRIA (1997, 1998a, 1998b) gives excellent guidance to contractors on waste minimisation.
[2] Egan Report (1998)

technology used. In some cases the additional transportation impacts of non-local sourcing may outweigh the benefits. Care must be taken to ensure that the proprietary system is robust enough to meet the local climate conditions of the site chosen.

5.2.3 Re-use and recycling

Both re-use and recycling have a major role to play in the minimising of resource use and waste. The European Protocol on Waste makes it clear that the preference is for reuse, which means using less resources and minimising waste, rather than more energy-intensive recycling processes which may consume more resources:

1. Re-use whole building (best option). see Figure 5.7.
2. Re-use components
3. Recycle components
4. Burn components to obtain energy
5. Dump components in landfill (worst option)

Current Scottish practice is to have recourse to the landfill option, rather than any of the other four strategies, with 92% of solid waste going to landfill[4]. This is unsustainable in the light of incoming EU directives on minimising waste and the increasingly onerous tax on landfill levied in response to these.

> **Did you know?**
> Reclaimed timber is often of superior quality to new timber because it has been seasoned for longer and has grown more slowly.

Figure 5.7 The best option of all is to reuse buildings (St. Peter's Court, Aberdeen, Castlehill HA).

---

[3] Ayrshire metal products supply steel frame housing panels (see Case Study No. 6), Filcrete Ltd supply a timber panel system called Masonite (see Case Study No. 2).
[4] SEPA 1996.

Table 5.2	Environmental impact of different waste management options				
Environmental Impacts	1. re-use building	2. re-use components	3. recycle components	4. burn components	5. dump components
1. Raw materials consumption	minimal some remedial treatment will be required	fairly minimal requires resources to prepare and clean	depends on processes	high component requires complete replacement some energy resources saved	very high component requires complete replacement
2. Biodiversity/ Flora and Fauna	minimal disturbance	minimal possible transportation impacts	transportation impacts possible emissions	potential toxic emissions transportation impacts	takes up precious land cover and displaces flora and fauna
3. Toxic emissions to air, water and earth	minimal unless building is energy inefficient	minimal possible residues from cleaning	emissions at recycling plant	emissions to air	emissions to earth and water
4. Water consumption	minimal	required for cleaning purposes	can be high depends on processes	minimal	minimal
5. Energy Use	minimal unless building is inefficient	minimal required for preparation	fairly high can be as high as original manufacturing requirements for certain plastics transportation	energy gain transportation	required to service landfill site transportation
6. Solid Waste	minimal providing demolition is not excessive	fairly minimal	depends on process	minimal	very high
7. Health impacts	minimal providing building is efficient and safe	minimal cleaning and preparation may involve chemicals	possible emissions at processing plant possible chemicals introduced to recycled products transportation	emission to air of potentially harmful compounds transportation	potential leakage of toxic residues transportation
8. Economic impacts	minimal restoration can help retain local economy	can be more expensive than new components additional labour costs for preparation and cleaning helps retain local economy	can be cheaper than reuse artificially low costs can help retain local economy if processing is local	can substantially reduce fuel costs for heating in the short term (will run out in long term if waste minimisation followed through)	increasing taxation is making this less economically attractive
9. Social impacts	preserves historical continuity and local knowledge in the area use of local labour	partial historical continuity and local knowledge in the area use of local labour	can confuse identity of materials (plastic "wood") can introduce new beneficial materials	can help reduce fuel poverty in short term	highly undesirable and unsightly

An informal economy dealing with re-used construction products already exists in Scotland with various salvage and demolition contractors (Figure 5.8) supplying both high grade and low grade construction materials and products[5].
In Scotland, timber, roofing slates and tiles, bricks and blocks in a low-cement mortar are all suitable for re-use and are often of a higher quality than equivalent new[6]. Current contractual practice and economics, however, do not always favour the re-use of materials.

One obstacle to the re-use of materials and products is the guarantee of fitness for purpose (Figures 5.9, 5.10). Where a material is to be used structurally, it will require testing for integrity. There is equipment available to carry out such tests[7]. Non-structural use does not require such onerous testing and visual inspection will often suffice. Certain insurers may, however, require stringent evidence of fitness for purpose. At present there are still no British Standards or building regulations covering the re-use of construction products and materials. This puts the burden of proof on the specifier who may be restricted by professional indemnity requirements. Despite these obstacles, specifiers have successfully incorporated re-used materials into housing products (see Case Study No. 3)[8] (Figure 5.11).

An important design principle when specifying re-used materials is to **allow time for sourcing the re-used material at the outset of the design stage and allow a degree of flexibility in the design detailing to accommodate what material is found**. This has implications for the programming of a housing development and should be borne in mind at the feasibility stage. It may be necessary to negotiate an extended design programme with housing funders in certain cases.

Figure 5.8 Housing providers can store materials for re-use either on site or in a special store.

Figure 5.9 Re-used door being re-finished to satisfy fitness for purposes.

Figure 5.10 Detail showing repair to reused door.

---

[5] Salvo is the national organisation co-ordinating re-use in the UK. Their web site is www.salvo.co.uk and their bi-weekly magazine contains listings of live demolition sites. Two main suppliers of re-used products and materials in the Central Belt area are Retrovious in Glasgow and EASY (Edinburgh Architectural Salvage Yard).
[6] Liddell et al (1994) show which materials and products can be re-used.
[7] Salvo can provide information on testing.
[8] One of the most successful in this field is the architect Rod Hackney who has developed several housing schemes re-using local brick and slates in Staffordshire. See also CIRIA (1999) for other case studies.

**Box 5.2   Waste minimisation in construction:
                   pointers for good practice**

- follow European Recycling protocol with preference for re-use over recycling

- ask contractors to provide waste minimisation strategy for construction process

- investigate use of prefabrication, preferably from local manufacturers

- carry out a site audit to identify existing elements for re-use and recycling

- re-use as many existing elements on a site as possible

- specify materials and products with the potential for re-use and recycling

- if a site audit reveals no re-useable materials, try to source re-useable or recycled materials from the locality

- strike a balance between sourcing re-used materials and the distance required to transport them

- long distance transportation of bulk items should be avoided

- allow time for sourcing reused materials and products in development programmes

- allow design to accommodate re-used products and materials in construction.

Figure 5.11 Bricks can easily be re-used in landscaping and the building (Glenalmond Street, Glasgow Case Study No 3.).

5.2.4 Water conservation

The need for water conservation is not currently at the forefront of most housing providers' or occupiers' requirements. Some rivers are, however, already at their limit of extraction (Figure 5.12) due to the increasing use of water by business, industry and housing. Pressure on water supplies is especially high in the drier Eastern parts of Scotland (Figure 5.13). Housing providers can respond effectively by minimising use of water. Where water authorities have no plans to meter water, meters should be installed by housing providers to raise occupiers' awareness of the amount of water that is being consumed and the resources required to deliver it. Real water savings can occur when occupiers pay for what they use.

Baths, showers and toilets use the majority of domestic water and are the priority for water saving. Simply specifying water conserving sanitary fittings can save up to 30 per cent of domestic water consumption. These can include spray taps, low-flush toilets and showers above baths or as a separate item from the bath. Power showers should be avoided as these can use nearly as much water as a bath if used excessively.

water consumption in dwellings

flushing the toilet	33%
washing machines	21%
baths and showers	17%
kitchen sink	16%
washbasin	9%
dishwasher	1%
hosepipes	3%

Rather than use water from the mains supply to flush toilets, waste shower and bath water can be used instead. There are now a number of proprietary systems available for recycling grey water (Figure 5.14) although they form a significant cost over and above standard housing costs and may require prior approval from regulatory authorities (see Case Study No. 2)[9]. It is not advisable to recycle sink water as this may contain toxic residues from cleaners and paints as well as excessive amounts of cooking oils.

Water conservation can also be achieved by collecting rainwater for drinking in areas with relatively good air quality. This has been carried out successfully in the UK but is perhaps more applicable to non-mains rural areas where spring water may be more unreliable and rainwater is cleaner. At the very least, rainwater can be safely collected from the roof in water butts at the base of drainpipes for use in the garden.

Figure 5.12 This river is at the limit of extraction already. Any additional consumption by human use will damage the precious ecosystem served by it.

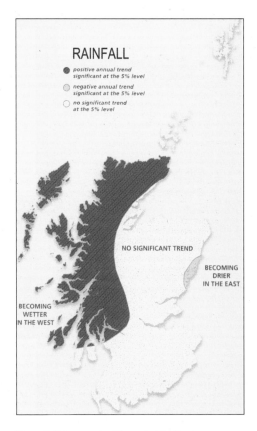

RAINFALL

● positive annual trend significant at the 5% level
◐ negative annual trend significant at the 5% level
○ no significant trend at the 5% level

NO SIGNIFICANT TREND

BECOMING DRIER IN THE EAST

BECOMING WETTER IN THE WEST

Figure 5.13 Some parts of the east of Scotland may experience water shortages. (©SEPA 1996)

---

[9] See Hall and Warm(1998) for a list of suppliers.

5.2.5 Domestic waste

Organic matter makes up to 50% of household waste. Given the intense pressure on landfill and the undesirability of incinerating waste, it makes good sense to encourage individual and communal composting of organic waste. Provision should be made on site for compost areas and these should be carefully designed for good composting conditions. The volume required per household is approximately 2m³. Additional provision for compost storage is also required in kitchens, ideally a small removable bucket size sealed container under the sink.[10]

Opportunities for recycling and re-use of domestic inorganic waste should also be maximised. This has design implications in terms of extra storage required both inside and outside for storing potentially re-usable or recyclable items until they are uplifted by local recycling/re-use schemes.

5.2.6 Sewage

Every day the Scottish population produces over one million cubic metres of raw sewage containing 110,000 tonnes of solid matter. The EU Urban Waste Water Treatment Directive to be implemented between 1998 and 2005, places severe demands on local water authorities to improve standards of treatment in an already overstretched system.

Housing providers have a useful role to play in minimising sewage discharge, particularly in rural areas where local sewage systems may be at capacity. The use of rural or suburban wetland systems with minimal energy input can

---

[10] See Roulac (1995) for an introduction to composting in housing. Further advice on composting requirements is available from the HDRA

Did you know?
The use of composting to reducing organic waste is growing. Aberdeenshire Council has planned to have all household organic waste communally composted within 5 years.

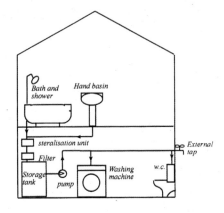

Figure 5.14 Proprietary greywater system.

Figure 5.15 Compost is already separated and collected in Germany. Housing providers should ensure there is space allocated for such initiatives.

Figure 5.16 Reedbeds can be used to break down sewage naturally in rural housing schemes (Trossachs Time Share Apartments - Watershed Systems).

minimise sewage discharge[11]. A wetland system consists of a number of treatment ponds which are filled with natural plants, such as reeds, that break down and transform the sewage into harmless compostable matter than can be directly applied to the land. There are already a number of schemes successfully running in Scotland[12] (Figures 5.16-5.17). Less intensive wetland systems can also be used to "polish" grey water which has been recycled or directly discharged from the dwelling. The result is clear water which can be safely discharged into the natural environment. Not all authorities accept wetland treatment of sewage and it is important to seek approval from SEPA for discharging the clear water into existing water courses.

Did you know?
Sewage is the largest single source of pollution of Scottish rivers.

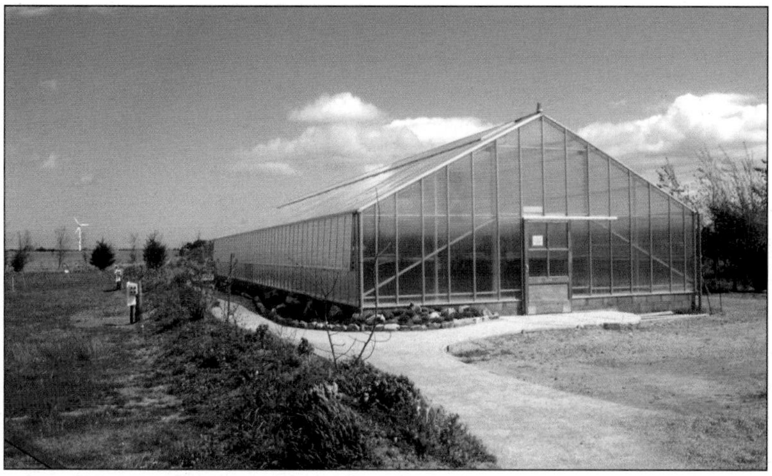

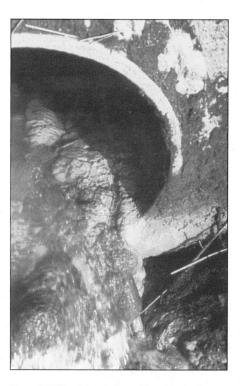

Figure 5.17 This natural sewage treatment plant serves up to 500 people and can serve rural housing schemes requiring autonomous servicing. (Living Machine Findhom)

Figure 5.18 The sludge discharged from this pipe is a by-product from the manufacturing process of PVC. Specifing low toxic materials minimises these problems, which are not 'visable' from the housing scheme itself.

[11] Grant et al (1996)

[12] for information on wetland systems in Scotland contact "Living Water" in Edinburgh, or Watershed Systems Ltd, Edinburgh. Alternatively, CAT (Centre for Alternative Technology) publish guidance on reed beds systems

Embodied Energy And Environmental Impact

The construction life cycle for housing (Figure 5.19) shows the different stages that need to be considered for overall environmental impact analysis. It is increasingly important to look at all stages of the construction lifecycle as housing becomes more energy efficient. Calculating the total embodied energy required to take construction materials and products through a complete housing life cycle involves:

- extraction
- production
- transportation
- construction
- maintenance
- deconstruction
- waste management

Calculating embodied energy is complex and usually omits maintenance, deconstruction and waste aspects because these are too site specific. Figures can only be used as an order of magnitude and usually only relate to the volume or weight of a material rather than the comparative amount required for the same building element such as a wall. No account is taken of the ability of a material to be reused. Transportation of materials also plays a significant role in embodied energy calculations where dwellings are remote. Nevertheless it is still a useful pointer to the overall environmental impact of a material or product.

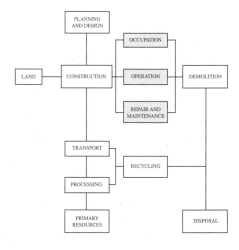

Figure 5.19 Construction life cycle for housing showing all the stages that need to be considered to ensure sustainable construction of housing.

Typical embodied energy of common building materials kWh/m³	
aluminium	103,000
steel	75,600
plastics	47,000
glass	23,000
imported softwood	7,540
clay tiles	1,520
bricks	1,462
plasterboard	900
concrete tiles	630
concrete	600
local slates	540
mineral wool (loose)	230
local softwood	110

The best approach for housing providers in relation to embodied energy is to employ basic principles (See Box 5.4) rather than generic lists of figures. Consultants should be encouraged to obtain embodied energy ratings from manufacturers where possible for comparison.

A more comprehensive analysis of the environmental impact of a material or product can be obtained from a full Life Cycle Analysis (LCA). Each stage of the life cycle of a construction material is examined for a number of environmental impacts.

> **Factors in Life Cycle Analysis**
> 1. Raw materials consumption
> 2. Biodiversity/Flora and Fauna Ecology
> 3. Toxic emissions to air, water and earth
> 4. Water consumption
> 5. Energy use in manufacture and use
> 6. Solid waste

Key issues at present in terms of environmental impact are preventing deforestation through unsustainable harvesting of timber and avoiding ozone-depleting materials in construction (Figure 5.20). Guidance is available on both these areas.[13] LCA is still a developing field and can seem bewildering to most housing professionals. There are, however, a number of very useful services and publications providing independent comparative environmental information on products which housing providers can draw on[14]. As with local sourcing of products and materials, housing providers should encourage consultants to build up their own databases on environmentally friendly products.

Figure 5.20 Specifying timber from unsustainable sources will result in barren land such as this in Scotland.

Box 5.4	embodied energy and environmental impact: pointers for good practice

*   demand comprehensive environmental impact information from manufacturers

*   use independent sources of environmental impact assessment where possible

*   treat embodied energy figures with caution and in terms of order of magnitude only

*   use natural, renewable materials as much as possible for lower embodied energy

*   allow for transportation, recycling and re-use factors

*   for the same product, local manufacturing sources generally use less embodied energy

*   use highly processed embodied energy products such as metal and plastics sparingly

*   recycled and reclaimed products have relatively low embodied energy

*   ask consultants to build up a database of environmentally friendly products

---

[13] for guidance on sustainable timber specification see Forest Stewardship Council Scheme which is promoted by the Forestry Commission and other timber associations.
for guidance on non-ozone depleting materials see Hall and Warm (1998)
[14] ACTAC (1998) Hall and Warm (1998) Anik (1996), BRE (1998) are all useful sources for comparison.

5.4

Longevity Of Buildings, Products And Materials

By increasing the longevity of buildings, products and materials, housing providers are effectively conserving resources that would otherwise be used for new construction and new products. There are three factors to consider for extending longevity:

- designing building elements to be re-used
- durable buildings, products and materials
- designing flexible dwellings (see Section 1.2.3)

5.4.1 Designing building elements to be re-used

Construction components are increasingly bonded together with glues, resins and mechanical fastenings that make it difficult to reuse or recycle them effectively. An example is the use of sandwich products such as insulation bonded to fibre glass mesh bonded to a polymer render finish (Figure 5.21.). These should be avoided where possible and a system of layered construction adopted instead.

Once design for sustainable deconstruction is adopted, existing components can be re-used in future developments generating both cost and resource savings. Timber re-use, for example, is greatly facilitated through the use of screws and bolts rather than nailing.

Where deconstructed materials cannot be immediately re-used, housing providers can set up their own storage yards on land designated for general storage purposes (Figure 5.22). These should contain any materials surplus to requirement which can then be advertised for sale to other developers.

Box 5.5	Re-use of construction components: pointers for good practice

Design whole dwelling for deconstruction using:

- small, easy to handle components

- modular sizing

- removable fixings

- robust, removable materials and components

- layered components rather than bonded ones

- identified storage areas for deconstructed materials

> **Did you know?**
> Some local authorities in Scotland already have storage yards for re-usable construction materials.

Figure 5.21 External insulation systems which are bonded together are very difficult to recycle.

Figure 5.22 Housing providers should insist that contractors reclaim re-usable items when demolishing or altering existing housing stock.

5.4.2 Durable buildings, products, and materials

Typically new build housing developments are designed to a lifespan of 60 years when they could easily be designed to last 100 or even 200 years (Figure 5.23). Refurbishment schemes often have an even shorter designed lifespan of 30 years, even though the building may already be three times that age. Using durable materials and products for housing reduces the amount of raw material resources required to service housing over its lifetime.

Tough, hard wearing and weatherproof materials should be used on the most exposed parts of the building in accordance with the local climate. Detailing should provide maximum protection of the material from the elements.

Some materials are inherently durable but also use significant amounts of energy to manufacture. A careful balance needs to be struck between these two factors to ensure minimum environmental impact overall.

Figure 5.23 Traditional buildings provide good examples of protection detailing and robust materials to cope with the tough Scottish climate helping them to last for hundreds of years.

Box 5.6	Longevity of dwellings: pointers for good practice

- design components and materials for re-use

- design with durable detailing

- use durable products and materials

- balance durability of products against their overall environmental impact

- design flexible spaces for changing spatial requirements of people living in them

- use principle of "lifetime homes" and design for requirements of all age groups (see Section 1.2.3)

- allow detailing and layout to accommodate users with special needs

- consider adaptation possibilities for ethnic and other minority groups with special requirements

Resource Conservation Checklist - Key Areas

- specify locally sourced materials and products (see Section 5.1)

- use performance specifications to obtain the precise goods required (see Section 5.1)

- minimise construction waste (see Section 5.2)

- minimise water consumption (see Section 5.2.4)

- provide for re-use and recycling of buildings, products and materials (see Section 5.2.3)

- minimise embodied energy (see Section 5.3)

- minimise environmental impact (see Section 5.3)

- increase longevity of buildings, products and materials through design and specification (see Section 5.4)

- allow for additional internal and external storage for composting organic waste (see Section 5.2.5)

- provide facilities for separation and storage of recyclable household waste (see Section 5.2)

- consider natural processing of sewage on rural/suburban sites (See section 5.2.6)

Chapter Six
Healthy Dwellings

The World Health Organisation defines health as "a state of complete physical, mental and social wellbeing". Dwellings can provide a stimulating and relatively stress-free environment that increases our sense of wellbeing. Poorly designed dwellings, however, increase ill health through unnecessary pollution and discomfort.

This chapter offers guidance on the following key areas so that housing providers adopt a positive approach to healthy dwelling design:

- interaction of the human body with the environment
- materials and toxicity in the home
- holistic wellbeing

6.1

Interaction Of Human Body With The Environment

Some key physical processes which influence human health are:

- thermal comfort
- humidity
- ventilation
- lighting
- sound

Comfort is significantly increased and tolerance levels raised when users feel they can adjust the comfort conditions of their surrounding. It is very important that housing providers allow any environmental control system in the dwelling, such as lighting, heating or ventilation, to have the option for override by the individual occupier. The design of the dwelling itself should also be flexible enough to accommodate this.

> **Did you know?**
> Allowing people to have personal control over the temperature in their indoor environment can increase their tolerance of lower temperatures and saves energy use

	thermal comfort	humidity	ventilation	lighting	sound
Table 6.1	**Measures to enhance human comfort inside dwellings**				
building fabric	ensure building is well insulated all round to avoid "cold spots" provide visible point source of heating (gas fire, woodstove etc) in living room -this has strong psychological effect of wellbeing on occupant	avoid condensation due to accumulation of moisture on cold surfaces use "breathing wall" construction to allow moisture to leave dwelling naturally avoid damp due to penetration of moisture from outside	prevent uncontrollable air leakage and draughts	avoid glare by allowing building to self-shade as required and design of fenestration allow for maximum penetration of daylight using openings in building fabric	energy efficient windows, particularly double frame ones with a larger air gap, have the additional benefit of greater sound reduction use careful detailing to prevent sound leakage through cracks and joints
air quality	radiant heat is more comfortable than convective heat mechanical air heating systems can feel very dry and uncomfortable -avoid if possible	avoid condensation due to accumulation of moisture in air use plants to provide humidity in centrally heated homes	quality of ventilation is important -avoid draughts keep above 0.5 air changes per hour to avoid damp and smells avoid mechanical ventilation if possible	Use sunlight to heat the air and give a pleasant warmth provide ventilation measures to avoid overheating	include external planting and trees in housing developments to encourage natural air-borne sounds and absorb artificial noise
material quality/ medium quality	provide materials that are warm to touch (wood, plastic, cloth) metals are cold to touch	use hygroscopic "breathing materials" to absorb moisture avoid moisture resistant materials internally	provide materials that minimise off-gassing into the indoor air to prevent air pollution.	provide daylighting which changes subtly over the day and comes from more than one angle, as this is restful and comfortable use natural shading devices such as deciduous plants and trees, to provide a gentle and changing filter for daylight in the summer while allowing more filtered daylight through in the winter	use the texture of materials and their different densities to alter sound qualities of spaces
user control	heating strategy should be easy to understand by the user	use humidistat extract fans to remove moisture at source and check settings	provide controllable ventilation that allows the user to increase ventilation as necessary	provide occupiers with dimmer switches to give control of lighting and save energy	provide means for users to ventilate house without compromising sound reduction in noisy areas

6.2

Materials And Toxicity In The Home

The strong chemical smell given off by new kitchen areas is an example of indoor pollution in dwellings due to off-gassing by artificial products and materials. This is set to increase as we reduce ventilation levels in dwellings to save energy. Often the initial strong smell wears off after a few weeks, but some products can continue to off-gas at low levels for many months.

Assessing the health effects of pollution is highly complex and findings are often disputed. In some cases, high level off-gassing by certain construction products and materials is a proven health hazard. The health effects produced by low level emissions, particularly in confined spaces, are less clear however, as are the "cocktail" effects of emissions from a variety of products placed together. Most disputed construction products and materials fall into this low level emission category. Although measured effects may be below the legal tolerance levels permitted, it is the cumulative effect over a period of time that can have adverse health effects.

Housing providers should adopt a precautionary approach where uncertainty exists and avoid materials and products that are disputed.

There is always an alternative product or material that can be specified but these may have a cost implication. Consultants should carry out a cost/benefit exercise based on suitable alternatives[1] (Table 6.2) allowing housing providers to develop an informed approach to environmental specification in their design guides (see Case Study Nos. 2,3,9 and 10).

The key pollutants that we need to minimise are:

- suspected carcinogens (cancer producing), mutagens (genetic mutation), tetragens (birth defects)
- Toxins and subtoxins (affecting bodily functions)
- Aeropathogens (including viruses and bacteria)
- Allergens (allergic reactions)

The first category is the most serious because cell alteration is often irreversible, and can pass onto the next generation. Examples of products containing carcinogenic ingredients include PVC[2] (which has restricted use in Sweden, Germany, and Austria) and certain timber remedial treatments[3]. Naturally occurring carcinogens such as radon, which is found in parts of Scotland, also need to be prevented from entering dwellings[4].

Figure 6.1 Clay and concrete drainage piping provides an environmentally benign alternative to PVC piping.

---

[1] Both ACTAC(1998) and Hall and Warm (1998) can help with sourcing and comparing alternatives
[2] Crump (1996) for a full discussion on the use of PVC see Hall and Warm (1998) section three. Also, Danish Environmental Protection Agency (1993)
[3] see London Hazard Centre (1989) for a good introduction to toxicity in timber treatment.
[4] BRE can provide advice on detailing to avoid a build up of radon in housing affected; the National Radiological Protection Boardwill test for Radon

Toxins are becoming increasingly present in the Scottish home through the use of highly processed products and materials that emit volatile organic compounds such as formaldehyde (Figure 6.2), organochlorides and phenols at some point during their life cycle. Some toxins are released during the manufacturing stage, while others are released directly into the dwelling. PVC products can give off lethal fumes when set on fire and should be avoided for this reason.

Viruses and bacteria are transmitted through organisms carried in dust and mould. These can be minimised by avoiding carpeting, keeping houses free from condensation and damp, and encouraging good waste management of organic matter.

The process of allergic reaction is still poorly understood. As well as being caused by specific pollutants and organisms, allergies can also arise once the body has reached a general "overload" point, having absorbed numerous low-level pollutants which combine to give a reaction.

Figure 6.2 Chipboard products can contain formaldehyde - a known toxin which can be released directly into the dwelling.

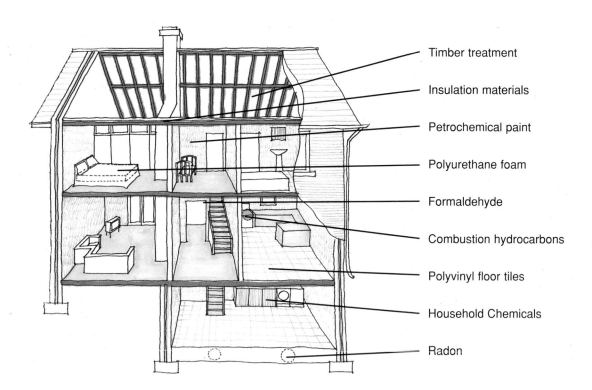

Timber treatment

Insulation materials

Petrochemical paint

Polyurethane foam

Formaldehyde

Combustion hydrocarbons

Polyvinyl floor tiles

Household Chemicals

Radon

Figure 6.3 The toxic house (after Pearson 1989)

Table 6.2	Potentially toxic substances and alternatives				
building element	disputed products/materials materials	toxic substance used to make product	health effects	alternatives	cost over standard specification
foundations	chemical dpc bitumenous dpc/dpm	organic compounds	nausea nervous system headaches	low odour chemical dpc polyethylene dpc/dpm engineering brick slate thin steel sheeting	additional cost no difference substantially more
structure	timber preservative	phenols copper –chrome - arsenic	nausea nervous system headaches	no treatment required borax impregnation	savings additional cost
secondary elements	timber preservative for windows/doors medium density fibreboard skirtings, linings urea-formaldehyde insulation	organic solvents formaldehyde formaldehyde	nervous system headaches nausea irritant to skin, eyes, respiratory system possible carcinogen	borax impregnation formaldeyde free mdf softwood non-foam based insulant	additional cost extra cost little or no difference little or no difference
fittings	chipboard kitchen units melamine worktops	formaldehyde resins (manufacture stage only)	irritant to skin, eyes, respiratory system possible carcinogen	wooden units or wooden doors only beech worktop	extra cost extra cost
services	pvc wiring pvc rainwater goods lead piping pvc underground drainage	plasticizers lead vinyl chloride (manufacture stage only)	carcinogen nervous system carcinogen	halogen free wiring HDPE (high density polyethylene) piping clay piping HDPE	extra cost little or no difference small additional cost
finishes	gloss paint varnishes emulsion paint solvents wood sealant adhesives pvc flooring fungicides	xylene toluene white spirit benzene plasticizers vinyl chloride (manufacture stage only) formaldeyde	nausea headaches nevous system reproductive effects carcinogen allergenic irritant to skin, eyes, respiratory system possible carcinogen	natural water or resin based paints and stains natural resin oil primer linoleum cork hardwood bamboo omit	emulsions -little difference resin-based -extra cost extra cost extra cost for natural paints

6.2.1 Timber treatment

Many timber preservative products contain hazardous active ingredients[5], which is why manufacturers recommend that buildings are unoccupied during application. Treatment is mostly unnecessary inside dwellings apart from fire protection. It is only essential externally where timber connects with the ground, or cannot be well ventilated to prevent rot. In some instances it is possible to carry out remedial treatment to existing timber using extra ventilation techniques (see Case Study No. 8).

Consultants should be encouraged to minimise the use of timber preservatives through careful detailing and specification of timber (Figure 6.4). Difficulties may arise, however, when attempting to get warranties from the NHBC or other bodies which require treatment certificates. In these instances, housing providers should source the least harmful treatment product. Borax impregnation is a suitable treatment in many cases.

6.2.2 Finishes

Solvent-based finishes should be avoided as much as possible. Water-based paints are preferable, particularly when they are natural based odourless paints rather than crude oil-based "low-odour paints" (Figure 6.5). Microporous and natural finishes also allow the surface of materials to breathe, increasing the ability for materials to absorb and emit moisture without deteriorating.

6.2.3 Indoor planting

Indoor planting can improve indoor air quality by removing up to 87% of the pollutants. The use of indoor planting has been proven by NASA (National Aeronautical Space Agency) to absorb artificial toxins such as formaldehyde and toluene. The most effective absorbers of toxins are the common ivy, spider plant and mother-in-law's tongue plants. Housing providers can use indoor planting beds in communal areas to improve air quality where this is appropriate (see Case Study No. 3). Planting can also be encouraged by building extra wide internal window sill boards which can allow plants to be placed in front of or behind curtains and blinds.

Figure 6.4 This housing has used untreated larch timber for cladding (Gledhill Leeds).

Figure 6.5 Some housing at Findhorn, Scotland uses natural based stains.

---

[5] see London Hazard Centre (1989)
[6] Reported by the World Health Organisation International Agency on Research on Cancer, (1989)

Box 6.1   Improving indoor air quality: pointers for good practice

- carry out cost/benefit analysis on alternatives to products and materials with disputed toxicity levels

- specify relatively unprocessed natural materials as much as possible

- avoid synthetic materials that give off fumes

- avoid timber treatment as far as possible

- correct humidity levels to avoid fungal growth

- encourage use of indoor plants which absorb toxins

6.3

Electromagnetic Fields (EMF's)

The Earth's natural electromagnetic pulse is essential to our health and well being. Domestic mains current operates at 50 pulses a second (50Hz) in Scotland, which is six times faster than the natural pulse, and studies show that this can result in disturbed sleep patterns, nervousness, and high blood pressure, particularly where beds are sited next to mains cabling[7].

Housing providers can encourage the building design team to minimise the amount of electrical mains cabling inside a house through efficient circuit planning. Circuit breakers allow bedrooms to be isolated from the electromagnetic effects of electric circuits at night. This is particularly important as we may spend more time lying close to cabling in our bedroom than anywhere else in the house.

Another source of electromagnetic disturbance occurs outside the house in the form of overhead transmission lines and electricity substations. Many existing housing estates in Scotland contain substations and many houses are within several hundred yards of overhead transmission lines. These fields are far more powerful than those generated by domestic mains. There is growing consensus among researchers that it is inadvisable to site houses near transmission lines, micro-wave masts, or substations. It is however, also possible to screen existing housing from the effects of these elements using thick concrete walling or equivalent material which can absorb electromagnetic radiation.

---

[7] see Coghill (1998), for an excellent introduction to this area

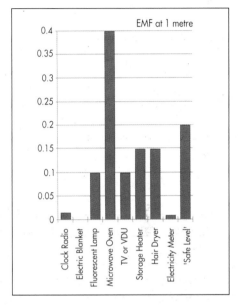

Figure 6.6 Some houshold items emit significant EMF at close distances
(After Borer and Harris, 1998).

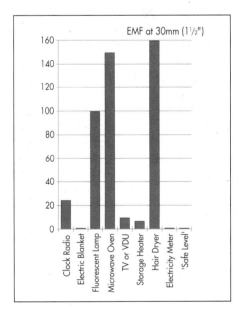

Figure 6.7 Microwave ovens can emit strong EMF's if leaking
(After Borer and Harris, 1998).

6.4

Holistic wellbeing

Our understanding of health in relation to housing is constantly changing to accommodate new knowledge. In the past, most emphasis was placed on quantitative health indicators but increasingly we recognise the subtle interplay of qualitative indicators. Table 6.3 below shows which issues are presently addressed and which still need addressing:

Table 6.3   Health indicators for design of dwellings

Current Health Quantitative Indicators	Sources	Additional Health Quality Indicators not addressed	Sources
Daylight	building regulation	colour quality of artificial lighting	manufactors building biology
Noise	building regulation and environmental health	life enhancing sounds	building biology
Warmth	building regulation	affordable warmth	poverty action groups
Dampness	building regulation	undue dryness	building biology
Air quality	building regulation and environmental health	electrostatic effects	building scientists building biology
Radiation	NRPB	Electromagnetic Fields	building biology
Material toxicity	control of hazardous substances act	low level pollutants quality of materials	building scientists building biology
Water quality	SEPA	water for emotional well being	building biology
Security	Police	User control	TPAS (tenant participation advisory service)
Basic amenities	building regulation	Contact with natural elements	London Ecology Trust Reforesting Scotland other interest groups
Community facilities	planning departments	sense of community.v. isolation	local voluntary groups community groups

Specifying appropriate physical responses to human health only partially addresses the issue. Health is a very subtle interaction between mind and body. Mental health in housing is as important as physical health and any technology introduced into housing must be closely allied to user requirements. This means giving the user control and understanding of the materials, products and processes used in their housing. This can be achieved through integrative and consultative management practice which fully engages with the user through participatory design and workshops with the consultants.

Housing providers also have the opportunity to address the qualitative aspects of healthy dwelling design and maintenance through user feedback. Incorporating health aspects into the post occupancy evaluation of new schemes can help inform future developments.

The use of sensory stimulation can contribute greatly to the quality of housing. Tactile, visual, and auditory stimulation all contribute to a sense of well being. This qualitative appreciation of the built environment and its interaction with the natural environment has been well covered in literature produced by building biologists and others[8]. Housing providers can encourage the design of developments that provide multiple stimulation through natural features such as water, trees, planting and wildlife. The gentle sound of leaves rustling in a breeze soothes while also providing a fresh smell and gentle visual stimulation through leaves swaying.

Figure 6.8 Planting can be introduced at a variety of scales to improve air quality in housing.

Figure 6.9 The provision of trees around our housing improves health in many ways.

---

[8] For a general introduction to qualitative health issues in and around the home see Pearson (1989), Holdsworth and Sealey (1992) and Day (1990)

Box 6.3   Holistic wellbeing: pointers for good practice

- adopt integrative and consultative management practice which informs the user

- provide clear but comprehensive user manuals, tailored to individual dwellings if necessary

- involve the user fully in the design of housing developments using tenant participation techniques[9]

- use qualitative as well as quantitative indicators in post-occupancy evaluation

- encourage design that maximises sensory stimulation

Healthy Dwellings Checklist - Key Areas

- specify non-toxic materials and finishes (see Table 6.2)

- take account of condensation and humidity levels (see Section 6.1)

- minimise timber treatment (see Section 6.2.1)

- use external and internal planting to absorb toxins and dust (see Section 3.4 and 6.2.3)

- provide adequate sound insulation while still allowing for natural sounds (see Table 6.1)

- promote holistic approach to user health using tenant participatory techniques (see Section 6.4)

- allow for maximum contact with nature in design of development

- encourage design which stimulates all the senses, not just visual sense (see Section 6.4)

---

[9] TPAS (see useful addresses) can advise on this.

Chapter Seven
Issues Specific To Maintenance And Rehabilitation

The environmental effects due to the huge amount of work carried out in maintenance and rehabilitation are far greater than the building of new housing. Although most of the principles and guidelines for the sustainable design of new build developments apply equally to rehabilitation schemes, there are subtle differences. Equally, the process of maintenance can have particular consequences for the environment if a strategy for sustainability is not pursued.

This Chapter provides additional guidance on areas specific to maintenance and rehabilitation schemes in the form of "at-a-glance" tables supplemented with commentary on key issues.

7.1

Maintenance Issues

Reviewing maintenance policy and procedures in the light of environmental consequences is an important step in providing a sustainable approach to managing housing stock. Housing providers should ensure that maintenance contracts come under the same scrutiny as new build contracts in terms of sustainable design and specification.

7.1.1 The myth of "maintenance free" components

"Maintenance-free" products often involve replacing the whole component if it breaks rather than mending it. A sound maintenance programme that allows for ongoing repair and care for elements of the dwelling can save significantly on embodied energy over "maintenance-free" products which may have a relatively short life. One direct comparison here is UPVC with timber windows and doors (Figures 7.1 - 7.2). Good maintenance of high performance timber windows and doors can ensure that they last over sixty years. UPVC systems can begin to degrade, deform or breakdown after 10 - 30 years' exposure to sunlight and can be difficult to repair.

Figure 7.1 An old timber door can be maintained and will be in place for many years.

Figure 7.2 A new pvc door will be difficult to mend when it wears out at key points.

7.1.2 Component lifecycles

Maintenance/renewal life cycles adopted for dwellings and their components tend to reflect mortgage terms (30 years is the most commonly quoted figure) rather than the actual lifespan of maintained construction. Components often outlast their predicted lifespans and are needlessly replaced on manufacturers' recommendations or on the basis of established maintenance schedules rather than through rigorous inspection of individual items. Significant embodied energy can be saved through accurate and evidence-based maintenance schedules which are demand led rather than predicted and provided for.

Table 7.1	Maintenance guidance for sustainable design		
site	**Resources**	**Energy**	**Health**
communal planting design land to be "owned" by individual occupiers effective maintenance cycle	**re-usable components** adopt maintenance policies that promote re-use of existing components use selective replacement	**glazing** keep it clean, otherwise you are wasting solar energy avoid using inert gas filled double glazing as it will leak after a few years	**non-toxic paints, solvents, stains and sealants** specify low-odour or solvent free products use natural alternatives where affordable
planting on buildings climbers may need pruning 2/3 years water source to be within easy reach	**check component life cycles** build up your own life cycle replacement programme based on experience of locality rather than theoretically	**embodied energy** ensure all replacement and maintenance products and components are as low embodied energy as possible	**timber treatment** avoid chemical treatment where possible provide adequate ventilation and eliminate moisture source
organic maintenance avoid herbicides, pesticides, artificial fertilisers to avoid health problems[1].	**local sourcing** build up local maintenance contractors and suppliers	**environmental products** build up database of environmental products for maintenance	**re-wiring** replace cabling with non-pvc alternative (non-halogenated cabling) provide demand switches in bedrooms
maintenance free planting use hardy indigenous planting and allow for wild planting areas to reduce maintenance[2]	**waste minimisation** ensure all maintenance contractors provide waste minimisation plans	**draught seals** are usually the first item to go on doors and windows - check periodically for airtightness and replace if necessary	**user control** provide maintenance manuals to occupiers and ensure that they are fully aware of the planned maintenance programme
evergreen planting needs less maintenance than deciduous with less leaf fall to clear up	**re-used materials store** build up maintenance store of re-used materials from old contracts	**gas boilers** use simple technology that is replaceable and can be effectively serviced	**ductwork and grills** any ductwork and grills must be regularly cleaned to reduce dust and potential infections
climate change plan life cycle maintenance for increasing storm damage	**water conservation** ensure all new bathroom and kitchen fittings are water-conserving	**renewable energy systems** may have additional servicing requirements	**user choice** allow occupier a degree of choice on replacement units where possible
	natural sewage systems need periodic maintenance to empty compost and other non-organic solids		

[1] Advice on organic maintenance of soft landscaping can be obtained from the Henry Doubleday Research Association (HDRA)
[2] Baines and Smart (1991)

7.2

Rehabilitation Issues

In terms of sustainable design, most of the principles covered
in Chapters 3 to 6 apply to the rehabilitation of housing stock.
The decision on whether to demolish or rehabilitate old housing
stock is based on a number of interrelated factors including
desired housing mix, density, suitability of plan form, and state
of repair (See Chapter 2). It is important to add the dimension
of sustainable resource use into this equation also. Demolition
always incurs the need for more resources than rehabilitation
and this factor should be balanced against the others to arrive
at a true evaluation.

Once the decision has been taken to retain a building, the aim
should be to fully exploit the environmental potential of the
building using environmentally benign specification and
minimising waste. There may be more restrictions with
rehabilitation than with new build in terms of exploiting all
sustainable design principles, but significant differences can be
made with simple measures like retro-fitting insulation.[3]

Table 7.2 outlines particular considerations for rehabilitation.

Figure 7.3 Glasgow tenement awaiting refurbishment © John Gilbert "Tenement Handbook"

---

[3] BRECSU (1995c)

Table 7.2   Guidance for Sustainable Design in Rehabilitation

Site	Resources	Energy	Health
site evaluation carry out careful site survey of existing micro-climate and note surrounding modifiers	**site and building audit** carry out careful survey and record all materials and components that can be reused or recycled from existing site and building	**glazing** avoid using inert gas filled double glazing as it will leak after a few years	**non-toxic paints, solvents, stains and sealants** specify low-odour or solvent free products use natural alternatives where affordable
passive solar check effectiveness of retrofitting passive solar sunspaces - avoid unless they can be easily built into existing structure (e.g balcony infill) alter window openings to suit 70/30% glazing ratio south/north where possible	**store and use reclaimed materials** store existing reclaimed materials on site for reuse wherever possible advertise material that cannot be reused or send to central store	**embodied energy** ensure all replacement products and components are as low embodied energy as possible	**timber treatment** avoid chemical treatment where possible provide adequate ventilation and eliminate moisture source
external porches add where applicable to prevent draughts and increase protection of main building fabric	**local sourcing** source locally to match original where desired	**insulation** maximise and use "breathing" insulation where possible avoid use of foams where possible adopt internal insulation where practical in preference to external insulation	**re-wiring** replace cabling with non-pvc alternative (non-halogenated cabling) provide demand switches in bedrooms
climate change check that existing details and drainage are strong enough to withstand increasing storm damage and rain.	**waste minimisation** ensure all rehabilitation contractors provide waste minimisation plans	**renewable energy systems** check orientation to see if active solar can be used	**user control** involve occupants in design and specification for rehabilitation
site history preserve significant components or parts of site which give continuity of meaning	**water conservation** ensure all new bathroom and kitchen fittings are water-conserving install meters where appropriate	**CHP and communal heating** consider this if existing layout of stock is compact can free up space in dwellings as boiler is omitted	**user choice** allow occupier high degree of choice on specification and layout where possible
communal planting protect existing trees design land to be "owned" by individual occupiers -split up site	**environmental products** build up database of environmental products for rehabilitation		
planting on buildings apply trellises to support climbing plants where suitable			

Chapter Eight
Financial And Management Considerations

8.1

Financial Considerations

8.1.1 Life Cycle Costing (LCC)

The life cycle cost of a house is defined as the total cost of that asset over its operating life, including initial construction costs and subsequent maintenance and running costs. Life Cycle Costing (LCC) is particularly relevant to RSLs since houses are durable assets for which the maintenance and running costs are considerable.

LCC can be used in two ways:

- RSLs are required to use LCC as an integral part of their financial planning[1]. Specifically, LCC is used to provide guidance on the size of the sinking fund that will be needed to cover future repairs and maintenance of their stock
- LCC also has a use in assessing the wider value of housing investment. LCC may reveal that higher capital investment at the outset will reduce maintenance and running costs, and that the latter savings will outweigh the initially higher capital costs[2]. This broader cost benefit approach is known as *whole life costing*.

8.1.2 Life cycle comparisons

The simplest way to evaluate different expenditure options is the *payback* method. Two examples are given in Box 8.1. In the case of the sunspaces the payback period is so long that the extra expenditure would not be worthwhile. In the case of the extra wall insulation, it may well be advantageous to spend the extra money given the relatively short payback period. A definitive judgement cannot be made, however, because the payback method takes no account of inflation or interest rates.

---

[1] Scottish Homes (1992); SFHA (1997)
[2] Flanagan and Norman (1983)

A major complication in using LCC lies in the comparison of costs. Capital costs are incurred at the initial acquisition stage and maintenance and running costs at varying points during the subsequent use of the building. Since these costs are incurred at different times they cannot be treated in the same way, "money today" not being the same as "money tomorrow". Future costs have to be discounted back to the present (or year zero of the investment period) so that like is being compared with like. Two approaches can be used equivalent to the two uses of LCC described above:

- choose a discount rate which will indicate the amount of money that will be required for future major repairs and maintenance. This will be the real rate of interest (the difference between the market rate of interest and the inflation rate for the construction industry) and is used by most RSLs in sinking fund calculations
- adopt a wider view and assess the value of present investment in terms of the opportunity costs of that investment. In the public sector, the Treasury recommends 8 per cent for investment appraisal purposes[3]. It can be argued that investment by an RSL is low risk and therefore 8 per cent is too high. A more appropriate rate might be that offered on low risk investments such as long term government stock. High rates of interest favour short term investment, low rates favour longer term investment.

Box 8.2

The commonly used formula for discounting future costs back to the present is:

$$S_0 = S_n/(1+r)^n$$

where:

S_0	=	the present value, i.e. the value of a sum of money at year zero
S_n	=	the value of a sum at year n (e.g. after year 10)
r	=	discount rate
n	=	the number of years

[3] H M Treasury (1991)

8.1.3 Whole life costing and environmental considerations

Sustainability is concerned with taking a long term rather than a short term view, and hence whole life costing is a useful tool for the financial evaluation of projects which are designed according to sustainability principles. Whole life costing for this purpose will differ from the LCC used for sinking fund calculation in the following ways:

• initially more expensive components are not precluded since over the lifetime of the dwelling they may be cheaper
• all replacement components are costed, not just the first (the justification for including only the first replacement for sinking fund calculations is that tenants should not be expected to contribute to expenditure from which they may not benefit)
• costs incurred by tenants are measured in addition to the housing association's costs
• the discount rate used will reflect opportunity costs of the investment rather than the inflation rate for the construction industry.

Research commissioned by Scottish Homes[4] compared the environmental burden and whole life costs over a 60 year period of an existing Scottish housing association development (the Control) with those produced by an equivalent development built according to a higher environmental specification (Ecotype 1). Not only was the environmental burden of Ecotype 1 smaller, but the whole life costs were lower also. The whole life costs of the two specifications are shown in Table 8.1 using two discount rates (the Treasury recommended rate of 8 per cent and the rate on long term government stock at the time of the research).

The following should be noted:

• Ecotype 1 has slightly higher capital costs
• even with the higher discount rate, Ecotype 1 has lower repair, management and maintenance, and running costs
• Ecotype 1 has lower whole life costs
• the occupier benefits in terms of lower running costs (heating only in this case)

---

[4] Ecologica Ltd (1996)

Cost Item		Control 1(£)	Eco-Type 1(£)	Eco-Type Saving over Control	
£	%				
3.88% discount rate					
Construction cost		39,167	39,602	-435	-1.1
Major repairs cost		5,221	4,556	665	12.7
Running cost		9,306	6,010	3,296	35.4
Management and maintenance cost		9,694	6,721	2,973	30.7
Whole-life cost		63,388	56,889	6,499	10.3
8.00% discount rate					
Construction cost		39,167	39,602	-435	-1.1
Major repairs cost		1,714	1,463	251	14.6
Running cost		4,101	2,649	1,452	35.4
Management and maintenance cost		4,272	2,962	1,310	30.7
Whole-life cost		49,254	46,676	2,578	5.2

Table 8.1   Life cycle costings of control and eco-type 1

Note: the major repairs costs are restricted to those building elements where the specification differs between the two dwelling types. This means that the costs exclude the replacement of common items such as sanitary fittings, kitchen equipment and electrical installations

This research and the experience of RSLs which have built to a higher environmental standard has shown that the most effective way, both physically and financially, to improve environmental performance is to increase the insulation in dwellings (see Box 8.3 which gives the costings for a recent development). This applies to both new build and rehabilitation. It is the simplest of the various mechanisms for increasing energy efficiency and is also the cheapest. Super-insulated houses can be built within indicative costs by making cost savings in other areas. Building at more than indicative costs can be justified in the long term, however, because the small extra cost incurred by the enhanced insulation is more than offset by the long term savings.

Box 8.3	Extra costs of higher environmental specification
Development	Tenement rehabilitation 12 units with high environmental specification (passive stack ventilation; extra insulation; "green" materials; sunspaces; condensing boilers)

Total costs	£626,000
Total cost of environmental enhancements	£118,000
Cost of extra insulation	£3,500

8.1.3 Policy implications

Taking the long term view, building to a high environmental specification not only reduces environmental impact but can also be more cost effective. The long term cost reductions are derived from:

- use of more durable materials and components
- reduced maintenance costs because dwellings are heated more effectively and hence suffer from less condensation and dampness
- lower heating bills for tenants.

There are strong arguments therefore why RSLs might commit themselves to extra capital expenditure to achieve enhanced environmental performance. If this has to be funded by borrowing rather than grant, there will be pressure to raise rents. However:

- because long term repairs and maintenance costs are lower, less money will be required in the sinking fund and this has a downward effect on rents
- occupiers' heating costs will be lower and this will potentially reduce the effects on their household budgets of higher rents. Some of the costs of the environmental enhancements may therefore be met from higher rents without disadvantaging tenants. Real increases in energy prices will strengthen this argument.

8.2

Management Considerations

The advantages of higher environmental specification are real but not automatic; their achievement requires careful management. In particular, RSLs will need to:

- provide education for tenants in the use of energy efficient dwellings
- modify procurement to take account of sustainability considerations.

8.2.1 Educating the Occupier

High thermal efficiency dwellings require much less heating than conventional Scottish dwellings, and to achieve maximum efficiency heating systems need to be operated in particular ways. Most new occupiers will have lived previously in dwellings with significantly lower energy efficiency and will be unfamiliar with the features of their new home.

In particular they may:

- keep heating on longer than needed and open windows to dissipate unwanted heat. This loses much of the potential energy saving
- use the energy efficiency for heat gain rather than cost savings. Where their previous dwelling was too expensive to heat to a comfortable level, this must be considered a legitimate choice. By using their new home differently, however, they should be able achieve acceptable comfort levels and also benefit from lower heating bills
- use their homes in inefficient ways thereby reducing energy efficiency e.g. putting carpets in sunspaces.

Prior to moving in, occupiers should be shown how their new home is different and given training in how to use it to best effect. This is particularly important where innovative systems have been installed (such as solar panels for hot water).

8.2.2 Procurement

Although environmentally friendly construction is becoming more widespread, it is still the exception rather than the rule in Scotland and the number of architects, contractors and consultants who have the necessary expertise and experience is limited. Housing providers should consider changes to their procurement procedures to ensure that they secure the required expertise. Innovation in housing may be incompatible with design and build as a procurement route for example. Scottish Homes has provided detailed practical advice on balancing quality and price in the procurement process[5] and this should be followed where a higher environmental specification is required.

For their project at Turner Crescent, Methil (see Case Study No. 2) Kingdom Housing Association used a competitive tendering procurement procedure which required contractors to demonstrate both an expertise in and an enthusiasm for sustainable building. The following steps were involved:

- the Association's approved contractors list was used and 45 were invited to express an interest in the project
- the 20 contractors who responded positively were asked to complete a schedule designed to assess their awareness of environmental issues and expertise in environment friendly construction. This included a request to see their Environmental Policy Statement (if any), their knowledge of

---

[5] Scottish Homes (1998d)

environmental building practices, and their awareness of wider sustainability issues such as local employment impacts and community involvement

- a short list of seven was then established on the basis of the schedule returns and these were interviewed.

Useful Addresses

Government departments and agencies with responsibility for sustainability:

DETR
Eland House
Bressenden Place
London SW1E 6DU
Tel: 0171 890 3000
http://www.detr.gov.uk

DETR
Sustainable Construction Team (policy)
Tel: 0171 890 3628

Scottish Executive
Victoria Quay
Edinburgh EH6 6QQ
Development Department
Tel:0131 244 0763
http://www.scotland.gov.uk
e-mail: ceu@scotland.gov.uk

Scottish Homes
Thistle House
91 Haymarket Terrace
Edinburgh EH12 5HE
Tel: 0131 313 0044
http://www.scot-homes.gov.uk

Scottish Natural Heritage (SNH)
Battleby,Redgorton
Perth
PH1 3EW
Tel: 01738 27921
http://www.snh.org.uk

Scottish Environmental Protection Agency (SEPA)
Erskine Court
The Castle Business Park
Stirling FK9 4TR
Tel: 01786 457700
http://www.sepa.org.uk

National organisations and professional bodies:

Association for Conservation of Energy (ACE)
Westgate House
Prebend Street
London N18 PTU
Tel: 0171 359 8000

Association for Environment - Conscious Building
Nant -y-Garreg
Saron
Llandysul
Carmarthenshire SA44 5EJ
http://www.aecb.net
Tel: 01559 370908
e-mail: admin@aecb.net

British Standards Institution
389 Chiswick High Road
London W4 4AL
Tel: 0181 996 9000
http://www.bsi.org.uk/

Building Research Energy Conservation Support Unit (BRECSU)
Building Research Establishment
Bucknalls Lane
Garston
Watford WD2 7JR
Tel: 01923 664258
http://www.bre.org.uk

Building Research Establishment Advisory Service
Building Research Establishment
Scottish Laboratory
Kelvin Road
East Kilbride
Glasgow G75 0RZ
Tel: 01355 233001
http://www.bre.co.uk

Building Services Research and Information Association
(BSRIA)
Old Bucknal Lane West
Bracknell
Berks RG12 7AH
Tel: 01344 426511
http://www.bsria.co.uk

Centre for Alternative Technology
Llwyngwern Quarry
Machynlleth
Powys SY20 9AZ
Tel: 01654 702400
http://www.cat.org.uk/

Community Self Build Scotland Ltd.
6 Gorgie Park Close
Edinburgh EH14 1NQ
Tel: 0131 443 7031
http://www.cableinet.co,uk/users/csbs

Construction Industry Research and Information Association
(CIRIA)
6 Storey's Gate
Westminster
London SW1P 3AU
Tel: 0171 222 8891
http://www.ciria.org.uk

Construction Resources
(alternative building materials)
16, Great Guildford Street
London SE1 OHS
Tel: 0171 450 2211

Energy Action Scotland
Suite 4a
Ingram House
227 Ingram Street
Glasgow G1 IDA
Tel: 0141 226 3064

Energy Information Centre
Rosemary House
Lanwades Business Park
Newmarket CB8 7PW
Tel: 01638 751400

Energy Saving Trust
21 Dartmouth Street
London SW1H 9BP
Tel:0171 222 0101

Findhorn Foundation
The Park
Forres IV36 0TZ
Tel: 01309 690154

The Henry Doubleday Research Association
Ryton-on Dunsmore
Coventry CV8 3LG
Tel: 01203 303517

Home Energy Efficiency Scheme (HEES)
EAGA Ltd.
2nd floor Eldon Court
Newcastle-on-Tyne NE1 7HA
Tel: 0191 230 1830

London Ecology Unit
Bedford House
125 Camden High Street
London NW1 7JR
Tel: 0171 267 7944

National House Building Council
Buildmark House
Chiltern Ave
Amersham
Buckinghamshire HP6 5AP
Tel: 01494 434477

National Radiological Protection Board
Radon Enquiry Bureau
Chilton
Didcot
Oxfordshire OX11 ORQ
Tel: 0800 614529

SALVO
18 Ford Village
Berwick upon Tweed
Northumberland TD15 2QG
Tel: 01890 820499
http://www.salvo.co.uk
e-mail: salvo@scotborders.co.uk

Scottish Ecological Design Association
SEDA Information Office
The Monastery
Hart Street Lane
Edinburgh EH1 3RG
Tel: 0131 557 2500
e-mail: sedainfo@aol.com

Scottish Solar Energy Group
Mackintosh Environmental Architecture Research Unit
The Mackintosh School of Architecture
University of Glasgow
167 Renfrew Street
Glasgow G3 6RQ
Tel: 0141 353 4740

Scottish Federation of Housing Associations
38 York Place
Edinburgh EH1 3EU
Tel: 0131 556 5777

Tenant Participatory Advisory Service (TPAS)
74-78 Saltmarket
Glasgow G1 5LD
Tel: 0141 552 3633

Trade associations:

Boiler and Radiator Manufacturers' Association Ltd.
Savoy Tower
Renfrew Street
Glasgow G2 3BZ
Tel: 0141 332 0826

Glass and Glazing Federation
44-48 Borough Street
London SE1 1XB
Tel: 0171 403 7177

Heating and Ventilating Contractors' Association
Bush House
Bush Estate
Penicuik
Midlothian EH26 0SB
Tel: 0131 445 5580

Council For Energy Efficiency Development
National Cavity Insulation Association
Insulated Render and Cladding Association
Draft-proofing Advisory Association
National Associaton of Loft Insulation Association
PO Box12
Haslemere
Surrey GU27 3AH
Tel: 01428 654011

Solar Trade Association Ltd.
Pengillan Lerryn
Lostwithiel
Cornwall PL22 0QE
Tel: 01208 873518

Thermal Insulation Manufacturers and Suppliers Association
Association House
235 Ash Road
Aldershot
Hampshire GU12 4DD
Tel: 01252 336318

Timber Research and Development Association
(TRADA)
Stocking Lane
Hughenden Valley
High Wycombe
Buckinghamshire HP14 4ND
Tel: 01494 563091

Energy rating organisations:

National Energy Services
National Home Energy Rating Scheme (NHER)
National Energy Centre,First Floor
Davy Avenue
Knowlhill
Milton Keyes MK5 8NA
Tel: 01908 672787

Standard Assessment Procedure (SAP)
Contact BRE

European and worldwide contacts:

Bundesverband Gesundes Bauen un Wohnen e.V.
Braunschweig
Germany
Tel: 00 49 0531 352851

BYGGDOK (Swedish Institute of Building Documentation)
Halsingatan 47
113 31 Stockholm
Sweden
Tel: 00 46 8617 7450
telnet byggdok.se

Commission of the European Communities
Directorate General for Energy DGXV11
Avenue de Tervuren
Brussels
Tel: 00322 296 56 17

Danish Building Research Institute
Postboks 119
DK2970 Horsholm
Denmark
Tel: 00 45 02 86 55 33

ECOHB
(European Global Network Ecobiology)
Generaladministration
St.Galler Str.28
CH-9230 FLAWIL
Switzerland
Tel: 00 41 71 393 2252
e-mail: ecohb@gibbeco.org

Rocky Mountain Institute
Snowmass
Colorado
USA
Tel: 001 970 927 3851

Bibliography

ACTAC (1998) *Green Building Digest* , Dept. of Architecture, Queens University, Belfast

Aldous, T. (1992) *Urban Villages: A Concept for Creating Mixed-use Urban Developments on a Sustainable Scale* Urban Villages Group, London

Anik, D et al (1996) *Hand Book of Sustainable Building: An Environmental Preference Method for the Selection of Materials for Use in Construction and Refurbishment*, James and James Ltd, London

Baines, C and Smart, J, (1991) *A Guide to Habitat Creation* Packard Publishing

Bartholomew, DML. (1984) *Possibilities for Passive Solar House Design in Scotland*, ETSU, Harwell

Barton, H. et al (1995) *Sustainable Settlements: a Guide for Planners, Designers and Developers,* University of the West of England, Bristol

Bell and Lowe (1995) *Report on the York Energy Demonstration Project* Leeds Metropolitan University, Leeds

Borer,P and Harris,C (1998) *The Whole House Book*, Centre for Alternative Technology, Machynlleth

Boyle, G ed.(1996) *Renewable Energy: Power for a Sustainable Future* Oxford University Press, Oxford

BRE (1986) *Domestic Draughtproofing: Ventilation Considerations* Digest 306, Building Research Establishment, Watford, UK

BRE (1990a) *Climate and Site Development, Parts 1,2,3* Digest 350, Building Research Establishment, Watford, UK

BRE (1990b) *Choosing between cavity, internal and external wall insulation* Good Building Guide 5, Building Research Establishment, Watford, UK

BRE (1993) *Low energy lighting in the communal areas of housing. Energy efficiency in the communal areas of housing in the London Borough of Enfield* GPCS086 Building Research Establishment, Watford, UK

BRE (1994) *Low Energy Domestic Lighting. The benefits of compact fluorescent lighting in housing – a monitored study* GIL020, Building Research Establishment, Watford, UK

BRE (1994a) *Continuous Mechanical Ventilation in Dwellings: Design, Installation and Operation* Digest 398, Building Research Establishment, Watford, UK

BRE (1994b) *Information Paper on Passive Ventilation* IP13/94, Building Research Establishment, Watford, UK

BRE (1995) BREDEM *(Building Research Establishment Domestic Energy Model): Background, Philosophy and Description*, Report BR66, Building Research Establishment, Watford, UK

BRE (1998) *The Green Guide to Specification: An Environmental Profiling System for Building Materials and Components* Report 351, Building Research Establishment, Watford, UK

BRE Scottish Laboratory (1998) *Impact of Climate Change on Building*, BRE, East Kilbride

BRECSU (1994a) *Community Heating in Sheffield* Good Practice Case Study 81. Department of the Environment, London

BRECSU (1994b) *Energy Efficient House Design-Exploiting Solar Energy Planning for Passive Solar Design.* GPG73, Department of the Environment, London

BRECSU (1995a) *Draughtstripping of Existing Windows and Doors* GPG 139, Department of the Environment, London

BRECSU (1995b) *Energy Efficient New Housing: Low Energy Design for Housing Associations* GPG79. Department of the Environment, London

BRECSU (1995c) *Energy Efficient Refurbishment of Existing Housing* GPG155, Department of the Environment, London

BRECSU (1996) *Providing Energy Advice to Householders -a guide for local authorities and housing associations* GPG 208, Department of the Environment, London

BRECSU (1997) *Passive Solar Estate Layout* GIR27, Department of the Environment, London

BRECSU *Housing Energy Management: achieving affordable warmth for social housing landlords* (SAVE)

BRECSU (1998) *Opportunities for electricity sales to tenants from residential CHP schemes* NPP 112

British Standards Institution (1990) *British Standard Code of Practice for Solar Heating Systems for Domestic Hot Water*, BS5918, London

Broome, J and Richardson, B (1991), *The Self Build Book*, Green Books, Devon

Centre for Alternative Technology (1997) *Tapping the Sun: a Solar Water Heating Guide* Centre for Alternative Technology

Centre for Alternative Technology *Components of Renewable Energy Systems* Resource Guide

Centre for Alternative Technology *Water Power* Resource Guide

CIRIA (1991) *Building on Derelict Land* SP78

CIRIA (1995 onwards) *Contaminated Land Guides* SP101 –112

CIRIA (1997) *Waste Minimisation Site Guide* SP133

CIRIA (1998a) *Managing Materials and Components on Site* SP146

CIRIA (1998b) *Waste Minimisation and Recycling in Construction Design Manual* SP134

CIRIA (1999) *The Reclaimed and Recycled Construction Materials Handbook* C513

Climatic Research Unit (1998) *Climate Change Scenarios for the United Kingdom*: summary report, UK Climate Impacts Programme Technical Report No.1, University of East Anglia

Coghill, R (1998) *Something in the Air*, Coghill Research Laboratories, London

Combined Heat and Power Association (1995) CHPirb *(CHP in residential buildings)*, Information pack, London

Crump, D et al (1996) *Sources and Concentrations of Formaldehyde and Other Volatile Organic Compounds in the Indoor Air of Four Newly Built Unoccupied Test Houses Indoor* Built Environment 1997, 6, 45-55

Curtis, D (1999) *Going with the Flow* Centre for Alternative Technology

Danish Environmental Protection Agency (1993) (English translation) *PVC and Alternative Materials*

Day, C (1990) *Places of the Soul* Aquarian Press, Wellingborough

Department of the Environment, Transport and the Regions (1998a) *Climate Change Scenarios for the United Kingdom* London

Department of the Environment, Transport and the Regions (1998b) *Planning for Sustainable Development: Towards Better Practice* London

Department of the Environment, Transport and the Regions (1998c) *The Use of Density in Urban Planning* London

Department of the Environment, Transport and the Regions (1999) *A better quality of life: a strategy for sustainable development for the United Kingdom* London

Ecologica Ltd (1996) *Life Cycle Analysis of Housing* Scottish Homes Working Paper, Edinburgh

Egan Report (1998) *Rethinking Construction* Report of the Construction Task Force to DETR

Energy Efficiency Office (1993) *Benefits to the Landlord of Energy Efficient Housing: Case Study 186* BRECSU, Watford

Energy Efficiency Office (1994) *Benefits to the Landlord of Energy Efficient Housing: Good Practice Guide 21* BRECSU, Watford

Energy Research Group (1994) *Energy in Architecture : the European Passive Solar Handbook*, BT Batsford Ltd, London

Energy Research Group (1996) *The Climatic Dwelling: an introduction to climate responsive residential architecture* James and James Ltd, London

English Partnerships (1998) *Time for Design 2: Good Practice in Building, Landscape and Urban Design* London

English Partnerships and the Urban Villages Forum (1998) *Making Places: a guide to good practice in undertaking mixed development schemes* London

Essex Planning Officers' Association (1998) *Essex Design Guide for Residential and Mixed Use Areas* Chelmsford

ETSU *Guidance Notes for the Implementation of Small Scale Combined Heat and Power* GPG 1

Flanagan, R. and Norman, G. (1983) *Life Cycle Costing for Construction* RICS, London

Friends of The Earth Scotland (1999) *Foundations for Sustainable Resource Use: A Strategy for Scotland*, Friends of the Earth Scotland, Edinburgh

Giradet, H (1992) *The Gaia Atlas of Cities: new directions for sustainable urban living*, Gaia Books Ltd, London

Grant, N et al (1996) *Sewage Solutions: Answering the Call of Nature*, Centre for Alternative Technology

H M Treasury (1991) *Economic Appraisal in Central Government: a Technical Guide for Government Departments*, HMSO, London

Hall,K and Warm,P(1998) *Greener Building:Products and Services Directory* The Green Building Press, Carmarthenshire

HMSO ,*The Climate of Scotland: some facts and figures*, Edinburgh

Holdsworth, B and Sealey, A (1992) *Healthy Buildings* Longman Group UK Ltd, Harlow

Johnston, J and Newton, J (1993) *Building Green: a guide to using plants on roofs, walls and pavements*, London Ecology Unit, London

Liddell, H et al (1994) *From New to Old: The Potential for Re-use and Recyling in Housing*, Innovation Study No.1, Scottish Homes, Edinburgh

Llewelyn-Davies (1994) *Providing More Homes in Urban Areas*, Policy Press

Llewelyn-Davies (1998) *Sustainable Residential Quality: New Approaches to Urban Living*, London Planning Advisory Committee

London Hazard Centre (1989) *Toxic Treatments*

Lowe, R, et al (1996) *Directory of Energy Efficient Housing* Chartered Institute of Housing, Coventry

Macpherson, G (1995) *Home -Grown Energy from Short-Rotation Coppice*

Pearson, D (1989) *The Natural House Book* Conran Octopus Ltd, London

Piggott, H (1995) *It's a Breeze! A Guide to Choosing Windpower*, Centre For Alternative Technology

Prior, J and Bartlett, P.B. (1995) *Environmental Standard*, BRE, Watford

RCEP (1994) *Transport and the Environment: Eighteenth Report* HMSO, London

Roger Tym and Partners (1991) *Re-use of Upper Town Floor Property,* Scottish Homes, Edinburgh

Roulac, J (1995) *Backyard Composting,* Green Earth Books

Rowley, A. (1996) *Mixed-use Development: Concept and Realities* RICS, London

Rowley, A. (1998) *Planning Mixed-use Development: Issues and Practice* RICS, London

Rudlin, D and Falk, N (1999) *Building The 21st Century Home: The Sustainable Urban Neighbourhood*, Architectural Press, Oxford

Scottish Homes (1995) *A community participation strategy in urban regeneration Precis No 29*, Edinburgh

Scottish Homes (1997) *Scottish House Condition Survey 1996,* Edinburgh

Scottish Homes (1998a) Reconnecting excluded communities: the neighbourhood impacts of owner occupation *Precis No 74*, Edinburgh

Scottish Homes (1998b) The development of foyers in Scotland *Precis No 73*, Edinburgh

Scottish Homes (1998c) Community based housing and local economic regeneration: a guide to the potential *Precis No 67*, Edinburgh

Scottish Homes (1998d) Housing Association Procurement Guide: Annex 5 and Annex 6 *Guidance Note SHGN 98/22*, Edinburgh

Scottish Homes (2000) *Scottish Homes Sustainable Development Policy,* Edinburgh

Scottish Homes (1999b) Fitting together? A study of partnership processes in Scotland *Precis No 98*, Edinburgh

Scottish Homes, COSLA, Scottish House Builders Association and Scottish Natural Heritage(1999) *Quality Greenspace for Residential Areas* (CD-ROM), Edinburgh

Scottish Office (1991) *Siting and Design of New Housing in the Countryside* PAN 36, Edinburgh

Scottish Office (1994a) *The Planning System* NPPG 1, Edinburgh

Scottish Office (1994b) *Fitting New Housing into the Landscape* PAN 44, Edinburgh

Scottish Office Building Directorate (1995) *Findings and Recommendations from the Scottish Energy Efficiency Initiatives*, Edinburgh

Scottish Office (1996) *Land for Housing* NPPG 3, Edinburgh

Scottish Office (1998a) *Climate Change Impacts in Scotland* Report of Workshop, UK Climate Impacts Programme

Scottish Office (1998b) *Integrated Transport: Travel Choices for Scotland,* Edinburgh

Scottish Office (1998c) *Report of the Community Planning Group,* Edinburgh

Scottish Office (1999a) *Down to Earth: a Scottish Perspective on Sustainable Development,* Edinburgh

Scottish Office (1999b) *Poor Housing and Ill Health: A Summary of the Research Evidence,* Edinburgh

Scottish Office (1999c) *Transport and Planning* NPPG 17, Edinburgh

Scottish Office (1999d) *Transport and Planning* PAN 57, Edinburgh

SEPA (1996) *State of the Environment Report,* Stirling

SEPA (1998) *A Guide to Sustainable Urban Drainage,* Stirling

SFHA (1997) Planned Maintenance and Repairs *Guidance Booklet* 3, Edinburgh

Smerdon, T et al (1997) *Sustainable Housing –options for independent energy, water supply and sewage* BSRIA Application Guide AG 26/97, Bracknell

The Stationery Office (1999) *Housing for Varying Needs* (Parts 1 and 2), Edinburgh

Wilcox, S. et al (1998) *Scottish Housing Review 1988-1998* Scottish Homes, Edinburgh

Selected Reference Material on Sustainable Housing Design

The following are considered to be core references for the sustainable design of housing.

ACTAC (1998) *Green Building Digest*
Still one of the best UK sources of information on environmental building issues, and well worth subscribing to. There are easy to read charts, which clearly assess products and materials on a range of environmental issues.

Anik, D et al (1996) *Hand Book of Sustainable Building: An Environmental Preference Method for the Selection of Materials for Use in Construction and Refurbishment*
An easy to read guide that offers sustainable alternatives to standard material/product specifications.

Barton, H. et al (1995) *Sustainable Settlements: a Guide for Planners, Designers and Developers*, University of the West of England, Bristol.
A comprehensive and detailed guide to the planning of settlements and the design of developments that achieve sustainability objectives.

Borer, P and Harris, C (1998) *The Whole House Book*
This well illustrated and technically detailed book on sustainable housing is rapidly becoming the bench mark reference for sustainable housing design. Covers individual dwellings only.

BRE Scottish Laboratory (1995) *Findings and Recommendations from the Scottish Energy Efficiency Initiatives*
Informative research, which compares the cost-benefits of different energy efficiency measures for housing in Scotland, based on a variety of case studies. Also includes a section on embodied energy. Highly relevant.

BRECSU GPG79 *Energy Efficient New Housing: Low Energy Design for Housing Associations*
A basic technical guide that elaborates on items covered in Chapters 3 and 4, on The Site and Energy Use.

Department of the Environment, Transport and the Regions (1998b) *Planning for Sustainable Development: Towards Better Practice* London
A comprehensive guide to sustainable land use planning with guidance on residential density and urban design.

Energy Research Group (1996) *The Climatic Dwelling: an introduction to climate responsive residential architecture*
A general introduction to the issue of climate and housing, with an interesting historical context which is still relevant today. Well illustrated.

English Partnerships (1998) *Time for Design 2: Good Practice in Building, Landscape and Urban Design* London
An introduction to the principles of sustainable urban design.

English Partnerships and the Urban Villages Forum (1998) *Making Places: a guide to good practice in undertaking mixed development schemes* London
An introduction to mixed use development.

Hall, K and Warm, P (1998) *Greener Building :Products and Services Directory*
Subscription based directory, which contains the most comprehensive listing of sustainable products and materials in the UK. Also has excellent address list for producers and explanatory background information.

Johnston, J and Newton, J (1994) *Building Green:* a guide to using plants on roofs, walls and pavements Beautifully illustrated small paperback which is packed with information on using planting sustainably.

London Hazard Centre (1989) *Toxic Treatments*
A powerful argument is provided against chemical treatment of timber with a comprehensive directory of toxic chemicals present in some timber treatment products.

Lowe, R, et al (1996) *Directory of Energy Efficient Housing*
Another "guide to the guides" packed with technical detail and references. Not highly illustrated, but a very comprehensive reference manual in an A5 format.

Scottish Homes, COSLA, Scottish House Builders Association and Scottish Natural Heritage(1999) *Quality Greenspace for Residential Areas*
A useful guide provided on a CD-ROM.

Talbot, J (1993) *Simply Build Green*
This book describes in detail one group's attempt to build ecological houses by themselves in Scotland. It covers the mistakes made as well as the successes and is an invaluable introduction to sustainable housing.

Case Study No.1
Urban Design for Social Sustainability

Crown Street Regeneration Project, Gorbals, Glasgow

Type: **Number of units:**	Mixed Use 659 owner occupied dwellings, 173 social rented homes		
SAP rating: **U-values:**	**various** **various**		
Fuel costs:	**n/a**		
Works costs: **Unit cost:**	**various** **various**		
Completion date:	Summer 2000		
Contacts:	Crown Street Regeneration Project New Gorbals Housing Association	0141 429 8956 0141 429 3900	

- mixed use development
- part brownfield site
- partnership
- high density
- sustainable high quality urban design
- community participation

The Crown Street Regeneration Project arose out of protracted community protest at the failure of earlier efforts to improve quality of life in the Gorbals through comprehensive redevelopment and mass housing by the local authority.

The demolition of the Hutchiesontown E blocks in 1987 made available a 16 hectare site close to the city centre and the opportunity for sustainable urban redevelopment. A new approach was adopted by the Crown Street Regeneration Project, the main aims of which are:

- redevelopment to produce a high quality urban environment
- integration of development with the surrounding area both physically and socially
- improvement of the Gorbals economy.

These aims are to be achieved by the adoption of the Urban Village concept which involves:

- mixed land uses
- social mix
- high quality urban design.

It was realised that a narrowly-based housing-led development would not deliver the required outputs and a wider initiative was required involving employment, retailing and other services, private and public. A partnership was established to do this involving:

- Glasgow Development Agency
- Scottish Homes
- Glasgow City Council
- New Gorbals Housing Association
- private housing developers

Figure 1.1 The project pays attention to existing urban scale and form br reintroducing the tenement block adapted for family living.

Key Features

Urban design

In 1990 Piers Gough of CZWG Architects won an urban design competition which was to result in a masterplan which includes:

- reintroduction of the tenement form adapted for family housing
- grid street system with the street as an integral part of living space
- blocks as the main spatial unit with communal garden at the centre of each block
- streets and blocks to connect to and address the surrounding areas
- Crown Street itself to be bustling local shopping area and the focus of the area.

Figure 1.2 The overall masterplan re-establishes the grid street system.

Social and economic aspects

When complete (summer 2000) there will be 659 owner occupied dwellings and 173 social rented homes. The aim is to produce a mixed community of existing residents, people with connections to the Gorbals, incoming groups on high incomes and families with children. There will also be retail units, a hotel, student residences and business premises, the latter using upgraded railway arches. Incubator office space is also planned.

Community consultation and involvement, of both existing and new residents, has been a requirement throughout the development process and is seen as essential to the success of the area in the long term. This has involved direct community representation on the Steering Group but it has proved difficult to involve the wider community in other than a formal and reactive manner.

Regeneration of the local Gorbals economy is to be achieved in the short term by the use of local contractors and the assessment of developers on the basis of their local employment and training proposals, and in the long term through the related Gorbals Initiative.

Case Study No.2
Local Sourcing and Partnership

Kingdom Housing Association, Turner Crescent, Methil, Fife

Type:	New build, timber frame, terrace and semi-detached
Number of units:	15

SAP rating:	97
U-values:	0.18 Wm^2C roof
	0.25 Wm^2C walls
Fuel costs:	£7.75 pw (predicted)

Works costs:	£854,137 total
Unit cost:	£56,466

Completion date:	August 1999

Contacts:	**Client:**	Kingdom Housing Association	Bill Banks	01592 631 661
	Architect:	Fife Council	Fraser Middleton	01592 416 414
	Builder:	Bracken Lea Homes	Tom Daley	01383 882882

The brownfield site selected is close to local amenities and ideal for passive solar gain, facing south with large sheltering walls to the south and west. The layout of the housing has been optimised to take advantage of solar gain by grouping car parking at each overshadowed end of the site (Figure 2.1). This also usefully separates cars from pedestrians. Car parking itself has been reduced below planning guidelines to 1.5 spaces per dwelling. The development takes the form of traditional housing with a mix of 1, 2 and 3 bedrooms.

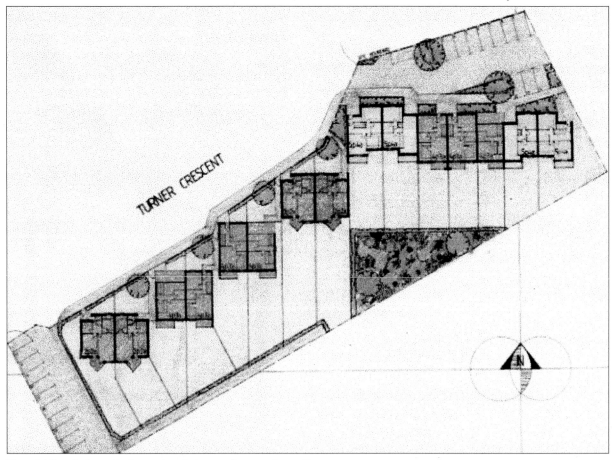

Figure 2.1 Plan of scheme showing passive solar layout and communal car parking

Key Features

Resource Conservation

Grey water recycled, water conservation, waste minimisation on site

A proprietary system filters waste water from the bath and showers before pumping it into a separate header tank which then feeds the WC cisterns. Spray taps, low capacity WC's, showers and rainwater butts all reduce water consumption as well. Unusually, the contractor was asked to provide a 3-skip system (timber, plastics, aggregates) which separated out waste from the site. Masonite timber I -beams use 63% less timber than normally required for the main structure.

Social and Management

Environmental audit of contractors, environmental management of Association, partnership

Two features which stand out particularly strongly with this scheme are the rigourous approach taken to selecting contractors on an environmental performance basis, and the actual environmental management of the Association's day-to-day activities. A traditional competitive tendering procurement route was selected for this project. The contractual audit consisted of a questionnaire which asked short-listed contractors about their environmental policies.

The housing association has a "Green Group" which promotes environmental practice within the organisation. This has resulted in an environmental action plan which has already reduced resource consumption in the office.

The housing association also formed a Partnership Forum which would generate a holistic approach to the design. This benefited the development greatly by providing advice on the environmental specification. The client has benefited from an arrangement with Fife Council which allowed it to obtain a good site at zero cost.

Partner	Role
Kingdom Housing Association	Client
Fife Council	Planning, design and donation of site
Herning Housing Association, Denmark	Expertise on sustainable design from leading country
S.E.P.A.	Expertise on water conservation and waste minimisation
East of Scotland Water	Expertise on water conservation
Forward Scotland	Expertise on resource conservation and energy strategy
Scottish Homes	Main funding body

The association has instigated a number of social "spin-offs" from the project. It is developing an educational resource pack for the local primary school as well as providing a site for a schools eco-project. The aims and details of the project have been disseminated to all tenants via a dedicated briefing process that will help to integrate the project's innovatory ideas into mainstream thinking.

Other Relevant Aspects

The Site

Biodiversity, porous paving, swale drainage

Porous paving blocks to the carpark areas allow surface water to drain naturally into the local water table via a drainage swale that feeds into a communal wildlife garden, preventing drainage surge in existing gulleys.

Energy Use

High insulation, solar panels, sunspaces, passive ventilation, micro-climate modification

Wall insulation: 170mm Warmcel Cellulose

Roof insulation: 200mm Glass fibre.

Sunspaces: the 1200mm deep sunspaces vent into both the bedroom and living space, maximising the benefit of passive solar heating. Service spaces (kitchen, hall, bathroom, store) are to the cooler north side while living rooms and bedrooms are to the warmer south side.

Solar Panels: heating for hot water is provided by solar panels on the roof which is topped up by a standard gas boiler in each house when necessary (Figure 2.3).

Passive ventilation: a proprietary system allows hot stale air to rise through ducts to the roof ridge vent without fans, reducing energy and maintenance costs.

Micro-climate modification: Heat-loss through the fabric has been minimised by reducing wind velocities around the buildings using a stepped layout to increase drag, as well as the use of planting and external structures.

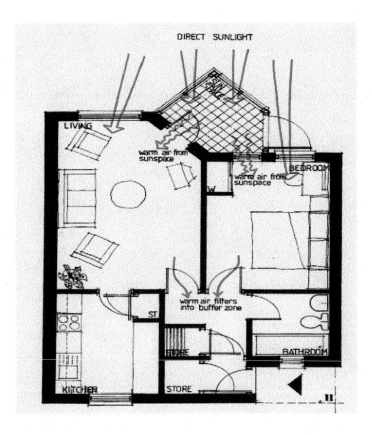

Figure 2.2 House plan layout showing passive solar gain.

Figure 2.3 Solar panels and sunspaces combine to save energy.

Healthy Dwellings

Local and sustainable materials

An environmental specification which sourced sustainable materials and products as locally as possible included the following:

- Clay common brickwork from local factory (reducing transportation)
- Filcrete Masonite Engineered Timber Frame (sustainably managed timber and timber waste)
- Warmcel insulation(100% recycled waste paper)
- Water based paints (low toxicity)
- Natural wooden floorboard finish (except kitchen and bathroom)
- Linoleum floor finish from local factory (reducing transport and low toxicity)
- High efficiency combined solar/hot water cylinder from local manufacturer
- Wood framed windows
- Natural clay roof tiles
- Natural clay drainage

Costs and Maintenance

Costs are approximately £10,000 per unit over standard costs. The scheme attracted £48,000 sponsorship in kind to offset the additional costs of the solar panels, grey water system, sunspaces and additional space. There will be some additional maintenance issues associated with the solar panels and greywater system.

Case Study No.3
Hybrid Renewable Energy, Reclaimed Materials

Shettleston Housing Association, Glenalmond Street, Glasgow

Type:	New build, timber frame, terrace housing and flats
Number of units:	16

SAP rating:	nomial 100 (160 calculated)
U-values:	0.14 Wm^{2}C roof
	0.22 Wm^{2}C walls
	0.22 Wm^{2}C floor
Fuel costs:	£1.80 pw (predicted)

Works costs:	£748,793 total
Unit cost:	£47,704

Completion date:	July 1999

Contacts:	**Client:**	Shettleston Housing Association	Nick Ronan	0141 763 0511
	Architect:	John Gilbert Architects	John Gilbert	0141 551 8383
	Builder:	Robinson and Davidson	Nicol Milne	01387 267423

The site is close to public transport and shops and sits in the middle of a traditional housing area in the east end of the city. The L-shape layout of the housing on this brownfield site creates a safe access and semi-private children's play area in front of a south-facing 3 storey block of flats and adjoining row of housing and cottage flats facing east and west. The scheme is almost car-free with only 4 existing on-street car bays and an individual bay for the wheelchair standard house. Privacy for the housing and front gardens is maximised using the semi-private space in front where car parking would normally be expected. The varied housing mix of 1,2 and 3 bedrooms includes convertible loft spaces, barrier-free standards and internal flexibility. This promotes the concept of lifetime housing.

Figure 3.1 Overall view of the scheme showing car-free play area, glazed atrium, solar panels and careful landscaping. Untreated larch cladding is used for the upper storey housing.

Key Features

Energy

High insulation, solar panels, geo-thermal power, pre-heated ventilation, passive ventilation, micro-climate modification, draught lobbies

Wall insulation: 160mm Warmcel cellulose
Roof insulation: 300mm Warmcel cellulose
Floor insulation: 75mm polystyrene

Combined geo-thermal/solar panel heating: heating for hot water is provided by pre-warmed water (12°C) piped up from an old coalmine which is 100 metres below the site. The water temperature is boosted by a heat pump and stored in a large insulated storage tank (10,000 litres). The temperature is additionally topped up by 36 m² of solar panels. The water is used to supply low temperature radiators (45°C) and warm water via storage cylinders. This is charged as a basic service charge within the rent for communal heating. Tenants can raise the temperature of the hot water if required using electric immersers which avoids the need for expensive metering controls. Low temperature heating is very suitable for well insulated properties and avoids risks of scalding by touch. Initial monitoring of the heat store shows that it is performing better than expected. There are many old mineworkings in parts of Scotland making this form of heating potentially accessible on sites situated over them.

Pre-heated ventilation: the carefully designed air-tightness of the dwellings allows for deliberate air intake through the void between the roof tiles and sarking using a small fan which pressurises the houses slightly. This reduces draughts as well as providing solar pre-heated fresh air using very simple and cheap technology.

Passive ventilation: a proprietary system allows hot stale air to rise through ducts to the roof ridge vent without fans, reducing energy and maintenance costs.

Draught lobbies: these are glazed and provided to the front and rear doors of the houses creating additional amenity space as well as a thermal buffer to the main building.

Micro-climate modification: heat-loss through the fabric has been minimised by reducing wind velocities around the buildings using extensive planting and external structures.

Resource Conservation

Reclaimed and recycled materials, waste minewater re-used

A serious attempt was made in this scheme to use as much reclaimed or recycled materials and products as possible and within cost. It should be noted that sourcing of reclaimed materials and products was time consuming and not always cheaper despite the obvious environmental benefits. The following items were successfully incorporated into the scheme:

- recycled newspaper for insulation material
- recycled wood chippings in the Truss Joist Macmillan webbed beams
- reclaimed brick from site for boundary walling
- reclaimed stone setts and paviours for front gardens
- reclaimed concrete paviours for rear gardens
- some reclaimed floor timbers (wastage from previous schemes)
- some reclaimed bathroom fittings
- some reclaimed railings from another scheme

Attempts made to source more reclaimed brick from Scotland failed due to lack of time and information. Cooled minewater discharged from the heat pumps is stored in a greywater tank and used to feed all the WC cisterns in the housing.

Other Relevant Aspects

Healthy Housing

Comprehensive environmental specification

The environmental specification has carefully minimised toxicological effects by specifying the following:

- untreated larch battens and cladding from Perthshire (reducing preservative treatment and transportation)
- calcium silicate external board panels (minimises vapour pollution)
- Warmcel insulation(100% recycled waste paper)
- timber windows and other external timber treated with water based preservative rather than traditional Copper Chrome Arsenate (CCA) which is toxic
- low odour paints and stains which are natural resin oil-based (no toxic emissions)
- untreated softwood cill boards and skirtings in preference to MDF (no formaldehyde)
- natural rubber flooring in communal atrium
- use of locally made bricks (minimises transportation and associated pollution)

Social and Management

Focus group to develop sustainable themes, communal atrium

Future tenants were identified and encouraged to join a focus group which developed some of the sustainable themes and gave a greater understanding of the issues involved. The group also participated in the choice of certain fittings for the housing including: showers, glazed doors, tiling, decoration, storage, kitchen units and floor covering finishes.

The south-facing 3 storey communal atrium to the flats was designed to encourage neighbours to meet and sit in the warm, pleasant environment. Internal planting beds have been provided to encourage communal planting with beds watered using only water provided via a communal tap (Figure 3.2 - 3.3).

Costs and maintenance

The scheme attracted sponsorship from Forward Scotland to pay for the grey water supply, solar air ventilation and solar panel system. All other costs were within Scottish Homes HAG guidelines.

Figure 3.2 Communal stair showing communal planting area.

Figure 3.3 A tap is thoughtfully provided for the internal communal planting areas.

Case Study No.4

Communal Heating, Community Inclusion

Elderpark Housing Association, Elderpark Street, Glasgow

Type: **Number of units:**	New build, timber frame, terrace housing and flats 14
SAP rating: **U-values:** **Fuel costs:**	100 0.23 Wm^{2}C roof 0.24 Wm^{2}C walls 0.40 Wm^{2}C floor £3.19 pw (predicted)
Works costs: **Unit cost:**	£699,075 £49,934
Completion date:	July 1999

Contacts:	**Client:** **Architect:** **Builder:**	Elderpark Housing Association Mike+Sue Thornley Architects Robinson and Davidson	Shirley McKnight Sue Thornley Alex Steel	0141 440 2244 0141 551 8383 01387 267423

Figure 4.1 Overall view of the scheme showing "room in the roof" construction and long life copper cladding to the upper storeys.

The site is close to public transport and shops and lies in the heart of a housing area in the south of the city. The courtyard layout of the housing on this brownfield site creates a sheltered and semi-private wildflower garden in front of a south facing 3 storey block. The varied housing mix of 1, 2 and 3 bedrooms includes room-in-the-roof design and barrier-free standards to promote the concept of lifetime housing.

Key Features

Energy

High insulation, communal gas heating, solar sunspaces, passive ventilation

Wall insulation: 140mm mineral wool
Roof insulation: 200mm mineral wool
Floor Insulation: 50mm expanded polystyrene

Communal gas heating: the most interesting feature about this scheme is its use of communal heating to reduce both running costs and long term maintenance costs. Two domestic gas boilers situated in a boiler room provide all the heating and hot water that the scheme requires via a continuous pipe loop through all the houses. Tenants are charged for this through a monthly service charge based on the area/floorspace of their dwelling. Additional heating can be obtained by the tenant using a separate immersion heater and cylinder in each dwelling. This minimises the amount of material resources tied up in the service infrastructure and reduces capital expenditure. The reduced heating specification is possible because of the high insulation levels in the dwellings. Although the engineer pointed out that radiators were only required in certain spaces within the dwelling, the association decided to install standard size radiators throughout to allay any tenant perceptions of inadequate heating provision.

Sunspaces: these are partially glazed and provided to rear of the houses creating additional amenity space as well as a thermal buffer to the main building. They are small enough to avoid being used as a heated 'additional room' during the winter months. The design efficiently allows two walls as well as the floor to be used for thermal storage.

Passive ventilation: a proprietary system allows hot stale air to rise through ducts to the roof ridge vent without fans, reducing energy and maintenance costs.

Figure 4.2 The sunspace is small enough to avoid being used as an additional room in winter.

Community inclusion through family support scheme

Future tenants were previously identified and included on the basis of a Family Support Scheme for the area which places families in need next to supportive families who are often relatives. Supported accommodation was also provided for people with mild or moderate learning difficulties to help integrate them more appropriately into the local community. The scheme strives to achieve a sustainable mix of tenants using a variety of different house types.

Other Relevant Aspects

Resource Conservation

Long-life materials

Copper cladding was chosen over other forms of cladding panels for the exterior walls to maximise longevity of the dwelling. It has a longer lifespan than zinc and other equivalent metals.

Costs and Maintenance

All anticipated costs were contained within an agreed budget with Scottish Homes. The long-life materials chosen for the exterior should also reduce maintenance costs.

Figure 4.3 The two domestic size gas boilers which supply heating to all 14 units are situated in a small communal plant room in between the two houses shown, for ease of access.

Case Study No.5

Passive Solar Energy, Resource Conservation

Fairfield Housing Co-operative, Lesley Court, Fairfield, Perth

Type:	New build, timber frame, tenement flats
Number of units:	18
SAP rating:	n/a
U-values:	0.21 Wm²C roof
	0.28 Wm²C walls
	0.45 Wm²C floor
Fuel costs:	n/a
Works costs:	£557,780
Unit cost:	£30,987
Completion date:	March 1999

Contacts:	**Client:**	Fairfield Housing Co-operative	Grant Ager	01738 630738
	Architect:	Gaia Architects	Robin Baker	01887 820160
	Builder:	Robertson Construction		01738 445123

The brownfield site is close to public transport and shops and lies at the edge of a peripheral housing estate. The "sunscoop" crescent layout of the housing creates a sheltered and semi-private garden area in front of a south-facing 2 and 3 storey block of housing. The housing is a mix of 1 and 2 bedroom flats.

Figure 5.1 The housing forms a curve to "scoop" the sun's heat into the centre and pre-warm the air in front of the block.

Key Features

Energy

High insulation, solar-orientated layout

Wall insulation: 100mm Warmcel Cellulose
Roof insulation: 150mm Warmcel Cellulose
Floor insulation: 50mm Rockfloor

A major objective for the client was to reduce fuel poverty in this scheme. There is a high level of insulation using a "breathing" wall construction that allows vapour to diffuse through to the outside. All electric 'Total Control' heating has been specified to minimise capital and maintenance costs. This is justifiable given the small amount of heating required and the future option of using alternative renewable sources of energy to supply the electricity.

Sunscoop: this is an unusual feature which optimises the layout of the housing to create a warm and sheltered micro-climate on the south side . The amount of energy required to heat the dwellings is reduced by raising the temperature of the immediate external environment on the south side. The combination of heat stored by the hard landscaping and the wall evens out the temperature over the day and evening.

Resource Conservation

Reclaimed materials and boron treated timber

Reclaimed slates were used for the roof, minimising embodied energy as well as blending in with existing roofing surrounding the site. Timber framing was treated with pressurised boron preservative as an environmentally friendly alternative to standard and more toxic timber preservatives.

Other Relevant Aspects

Social and Management

Continuity and community

The scheme is the product of a working relationship between the client and architect stretching back over ten years and many project phases; it contains all the shared knowledge built up over that time.

Costs and Maintenance

All anticipated costs were contained within an agreed budget with Scottish Homes. A HAG rate of 74% was achieved. Landscape maintenance has been minimised by subdividing backcourts into small private gardens.

Figure 5.2 Timber was treated using water based paints and stains.

Case Study No.6

Innovative Prefabrication, Lifetime Home and Local Sourcing

West of Scotland Housing Association, Mainholm Road, Ayr

Type:	New build, steel frame, terrace and semi-detached
Number of units:	20
SAP rating:	**114**
U-values:	**0.1-0.21 Wm^{2}C roof**
	0.17 Wm^{2}C walls
	0.23-0.25 Wm^{2}C floor
Fuel costs:	**£0.75 pw (predicted)**
Works costs:	£875,500
Unit cost:	£43,750
Completion date:	September 1999

Contacts:				
	Client:	West of Scotland Housing Association	Fiona Birse	0141 553 1413
	Architect:	Assist Architects	Monica McGhee	0141 554 0505
	Builder:	Robinson and Davidson	Alex Steel	0141 332 8837

The site selected was a semi-rural greenfield one on the edge of the town within reasonable distance of local amenities. Despite the awkward shape and confined nature of the site 75% of the dwellings benefit from passive solar gain. The whole development is barrier free and car parking satisfies barrier free requirements. The housing has a traditional mix of 1,2,and 3 bedrooms.

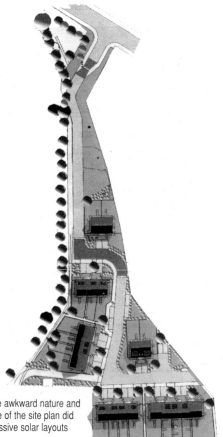

Figure 6.1 The awkward nature and confined shape of the site plan did not prevent passive solar layouts for housing.

Key Features

Resource Conservation

Pre-fabricated construction, local sourcing

The housing is uniquely manufactured from galvanised steel panels which make up the walls, floor and roof structure. The partnership formed between the client, the builder and a local steel fabrication plant (Ayrshire Metals) has helped this housing development to contribute considerably to the local economy. The technology of steel housing has developed since earlier versions in the 1970's and this system now offers the following advantages:

- faster construction
- accurate sizing which reduces waste
- lightweight for easy handling
- flexible and adaptable system for lifetime homes
- high acoustic and thermal insulation
- fire and insect resistant
- fully recyclable and re-useable
- advanced technology of protecting steel with "self-healing" coating
- "breathing wall" construction allows moisture to escape but with low air leakage rate

Figure 6.2 Steel construction increases efficiency in housing construction.

Social and Management

Lifetime homes, contractual partnership

Each dwelling is designed to be highly flexible and adaptable over time to allow for disability needs. There is a "knock -out" panel in the bathroom to allow for future fitting of a hoist as well as additional space to allow for wheelchair use. Services have been accommodated in the ceiling void or external wall thickness to allow changes to be made to the layout.

The use of a partnership arrangement from the outset between the client, builder, architect and steel fabricator has resulted in highly constructive management of problems with joint solutions provided. The traditional pitfall of the design and build post tender savings exercise has been avoided.

Figure 6.3 Solar porches as entrances help reduce air leakage.

Other Relevant Aspects

The Site

Shelterbelt, indigenous planting

The site has a continuous row of mature trees which have been both preserved and enhanced with new planting. This provides good shelter for the site from prevailing westerly winds. Existing planting has been maintained where possible and enhanced with indigenous species to promote appropriate biodiversity.

Energy

High insulation, passive ventilation, solar porches, mechanical heat recovery system

Wall insulation: 150 mm Rockwool quilt and 75 mm Flax/Rockwool "Heraklith" boarding
Roof insulation: 300 mm Rockwool to loft
Floor insulation: 75 mm Jablite polystyrene boarding
Solar porches are single glazed and narrow to prevent their use as another room. They provide an effective draught lobby to the main house and a small amount of pre-heated ventilation.
Exceptionally high insulation levels have been achieved by overcladding the steel frame with insulation boards as well as filling the structural void. Passive ventilation has been used on the 14 houses which have condensing boiler heating systems. In an attempt to overcome traditional oversizing of boilers in relation to well insulated housing, 6 of the houses use a mechanical heat recovery system as an alternative. This has significantly reduced the size of the boiler which is now needed for hot water only.

Costs and Maintenance

Costs for this scheme are within an agreed budget with Scottish Homes and relatively low given the innovative nature of the construction. Considerable space has been gained by increasing the efficiency of the structure. No cavity is required in the wall construction and the flax-covered external insulation board can receive render directly, simplifying much of the detailing.

Case Study No.7

Energy Saving Rehabilitation, Ecological Specification of Materials

Meadowside and Thornwood Housing Association
589-597 Dumbarton Road, Glasgow

Type:	Rebabilitation, Victorian Tenement
Number of units:	12
SAP rating:	92
U-values:	0.17 Wm^{2}C roof
	0.33 Wm^{2}C walls
	n/a Wm^{2}C floor
Fuel costs:	£2.75 pw (predicted)
Works costs:	£626,100
Unit cost:	£52,175
Completion date:	January 2000

Contacts:	**Client:**	Meadowside and Thornwood Housing Association	Neil Whitelaw	0141 357 3200
	Architect:	Murray Design Group	Ronnie Murray	0141 339 3472
	Builder:	Melville Dundas	Roy Paterson	0141 883 1155

The client for this scheme wished to set a replicable "green template" for rehabilitation schemes and has introduced a variety of measures more usually associated with new build. The existing tenement block has been wholly retained, sustaining a rich and dense urban fabric while at the same time minimising resource use. Car parking is minimal and access to all local facilities is excellent.

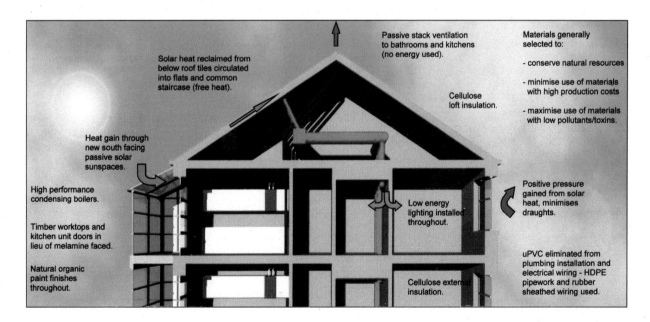

Figure 7.1 A number of innovatory techniques have been incorporated into this tenement rehabilitation scheme.

Key Features

Energy

Solar ventilation through tiles, passive stack ventilation, passive solar extensions, high insulation for refurbishment, condensing boilers, low energy lighting

Wall insulation: 100mm cellulose fibre
Roof insulation: 200mm cellulose fibre
Passive solar extensions: these are 1000mm deep and cover almost a third of the rear south facing elevation, providing extra amenity space, protection of the existing fabric and a thermal "buffer zone".
Solar ventilation through tiles: air warmed by the sun on the roof tiles is used to ventilate the flats and common staircase using very low wattage fans. The positive pressure generated by the fans minimises draughts.
Passive stack ventilation: this is collected via individual stacks from the bathroom and kitchen and taken out through the roof.
High insulation: the internal dry-lining of the flats is separated from the existing external wall using standard timber framing. The generous size of existing rooms meant that drylining had little impact in terms of lost space. Retrofitting a high level of loft insulation was relatively straightforward.
Condensing boilers: these are probably not necessary and could be deemed an overspecification. Communal heating was not an option for the client, however, as half of the residents are owner occupiers. The radiators have been deliberately sized large to ensure efficient running of the boilers.
Low energy lighting: low energy light bulbs supplied to each room reduce energy consumption from lighting by 80%.

Healthy Dwellings

Ecological specification of materials, "breathing" insulation strategy

A thorough environmental appraisal and life cycle costing on materials and products has substantially improved the standard specification for tenement rehabilitation.

Standard specification	Environmental specification	Rationale
Polyethelyne insulation	Cellulose loose-fill insulation	Allows building to "breathe" more, recycles newspaper, low embodied energy
150 mm roof insulation	200 mm roof insulation	Saves energy
50 mm wall insulation	100 mm wall insulation	Cost-benefit
Structurally certified timber	Forest Stewardship Council certified timber	Sustainable forest sourcing
UPVC above ground drain pipes	HDPE (high density polyethylene) drain pipes	Phase out use of uPVC
PVC electric cabling	LSV (polyethylene) cabling	Phase out use of PVC
Copper pipework	HDPE pipework	Saves embodied energy
MR Chipboard flooring	MR Formaldehyde free chipboard	Avoids offgassing of toxins in formaldehyde
Melamine faced kitchen units	Solid timber door and drawer fronts	Avoids pollutant and melamine facing which impedes waste disposal
Melamine faced chipboard kitchen worktops	Solid beech worktops	Avoids pollutant and melamine facing which impedes waste disposal
CCA timber treatment	Borate timber treatment	Avoids toxins
Solvent paints	Natural water based paints	Avoids carcinogens
Chemical solvent DPC and timber treatment	"low odour" DPC and timber treatment	Reduces toxins

Other Relevant Aspects

Costs and maintenance

The funding for this scheme attracted 90% HAG because acquisitions were very high. In addition the two bedroom units were roughly £10,000 over the cost of a normal two bedroom unit (£40,000). The passive solar extensions, hot water heating system and solar tile heating are the biggest on-costs. Extra insulation, borax treatment and the use of HDPE drainage piping instead of uPVC represent the lowest on costs. Predicted simple payback on most energy measures ranges between 8-14 years. The passive solar extensions do not offer a suitable energy payback over the predicted life of the building.

The contractor prices were generally high suggesting that a "comfort zone" had been built in to deal with the innovative aspects of the specification. The client may consider recovering additional costs by offsetting the rents against the energy savings in future schemes.

Case Study No.8
Rehabilitation without Timber Treatment, Landscaping
Fairfield Housing Co-operative, Phase 3, Fairfield Estate, Perth

Type:	Rehabilitation, tenement flats			
Number of units:	53			
SAP rating:	**Pre-SAP**			
U-values:	**0.17 Wm^{2}C roof**			
	0.3 Wm^{2}C walls			
	0.3 Wm^{2}C floor			
Fuel costs:	n/a			
Works costs:	£1,998,445			
Unit cost:	£37,706			
Completion date:	1992			
Contacts:	**Client:**	Fairfield Housing Co-operative	Grant Ager	01738 630738
	Architect:	Gaia Architects	Howard Liddell	0131 557 9191
	Builder:	Hall and Tawse, Scotland Ltd		01224 6931550

The rehabilitated tenement block, built in 1936, is close to public transport and shops and lies at the heart of a peripheral housing estate. The scheme is Phase 3 out of the seven phases completed so far. The layout and mix have been altered to build in greater diversity resulting in 1, 2 and 3 bed flats.

Figure 8.1 Extensive low level beech hedging is easy to maintain and provides an effective micro-climate when combined with taller indigenous trees.

Figure 8.2 The dense planting gives significant shelter to the housing and provides "free" insulation to the walls.

Key Features

Healthy Dwellings

Natural timber treatment and environmental specification

Timber preservative treatment has been avoided in the roof by significantly increasing the amount of ventilation going through the roof void which prevents moisture accumulating and causing rot. This treats the cause of the problem rather than the symptom which is the rot itself. The timber preservation consultants, Hutton and Rostron Ltd[1] carried out an extensive rot survey before recommending this measure after all existing rot was removed.

All internal and external finishes are non-toxic with timber frame windows specified throughout.

The Site

Landscaping and extensive micro-climate modification

A major feature of the rehabilitation of the whole estate was the comprehensive landscaping and planting of communal spaces and streetscape at the beginning. The planting of indigenous tree species such as rowan, together with deep beech hedging and other defensive planting has resulted in a significantly more sheltered micro-climate which helps to reduce energy costs as well as creating a high quality amenity space providing cleaner, fresher air due to the oxygenation and particle filtration of the planting.

---

[1] Hutton and Rostron Environmental Investigations Ltd. use unique investigation and treatment measures to minimise disturbance to the building fabric. Netley House, Gormshall, Surrey GU5 9QA
Tel: 01483 203221

Other Relevant Aspects

Energy

High insulation

Wall insulation: 100mm Rockwool
Roof insulation: 200mm Rockwool

A major objective for the client was to reduce fuel poverty in this scheme. Insulation has been added internally to all external walls. All-electric 'Total Control' heating has been specified to minimise capital and maintenance costs. This is justifiable given the small amount of heating required and the future option of using alternative renewable sources of energy to supply the electricity.

Resource Conservation

Minimum specification for maximum gain

The specification for internal insulation not only saves on capital costs but also significantly reduces the embodied energy tied up in the rehabilitation work by omitting insulated overcladding with its associated high energy costs. Externally, the renderwork has been carefully surveyed and patched only where necessary. A vibrant coat of paint has lifted the exterior appearance without the need of extensive re-modelling of the facade.

Social and Management

Community commitment

Fairfield Housing Co-operative was formed to take over 300 houses from Scottish Homes in 1989. It has a very strong tenant-run committee which is democratically elected. The small number of staff servicing the co-operative work out of an office in a converted flat in the middle of the co-operative housing. This has resulted in a very close working relationship between management and tenants with the result that the estate has developed a distinctive community feeling with very low turnover of tenancies, demonstrating high satisfaction. The tenants' committee has been committed from the outset to high environmental standards after an initial visit to other environmental buildings to see for themselves what could be achieved, and encouragement from their architects.

Costs and Maintenance

All anticipated costs were contained with an agreed budget with Scottish Homes. Although there are some additional maintenance costs associated with the soft landscaping, these have been minimised using easy to care for planting, and justified on grounds of quality of space and health and wellbeing. Redundant chimneys were either removed to reduce maintenance costs or re-used for ventilation purposes.

Case Study No.9
Rehabilitation, Energy, Tenant Choice and Participation

James Nisbet Street Housing Co-operative
James Nisbet Street Phases 1-3, Glasgow

Type:	Rehabilitation, tenement flats, 4 storey
Number of units:	Phase 1 45
	Phase 2 56
	Phase 3 44

SAP rating:	n/a
U-values:	0.2 Wm^{2}C roof
	0.42 Wm^{2}C walls
	floor n/a
Fuel costs:	£7.75 pw (predicted)

Works costs:	Phase 1: £1,352,000	Phase 2: £1,840,000	Phase 3 £1,702,000
Unit cost:	£30,000	£32,857	£38,682

Completion date:	Phase 1: 1991	Phase 2: 1992	Phase 3: 1994

Contacts:	**Client:**	James Nisbet Housing Co-operative	Laurence'O'Boyle	0141 552 7928
	Architect:	Assist Architects	Andy Jack	0131 555 5700
	Builder:	Tarmac Construction		

In 1989, James Nisbet Street Co-operative inherited 200 tenement dwellings built by Glasgow City Council in the 1960's. The housing is part of a large estate to the north of the city centre on a relatively exposed south-facing hillside. Amenities within the local area are basic but there are some public transport links. Car parking is well below planning guidelines. A decision was taken to rehabilitate all the stock, exploiting passive solar gain where possible and adapting layouts to form a more suitable housing mix.

Figure 9.1 Solar sunspaces offer a "thermal buffer" zone to the main flats.

121

Key Features

Balcony sunspaces, reduced north windows, condensing boilers, overcladding

Wall insulation: 50mm Rockwool
Loft insulation: 150mm Glass fibre
Sunspaces: in Phases 2 and 3, 1200mm deep south and west facing balconies have been glazed in to make very cost effective sunspaces. Thermal mass is provided by the existing balcony structure. They are vented into the living space, and pre-warmed air is casually dragged through the dwelling by means of humidistat fans in the north-facing service spaces. In Phases 1 and 2 oversized north facing windows were reduced to save heat loss. Condensing boilers were used in Phases 2 and 3. Overcladding insulation has prevented cold bridging.

Social and Management

Tenant choice and participation

A major aspect of the rehabilitation work was the close relationship formed by the housing management team and architects with the existing tenants. As a result tenants have a strong sense of "owning" the area and property they live in.

Tenant Choice: an initial social survey was carried out to find out tenant requirements and aspirations and a new housing mix designed to accommodate these. Every household was interviewed individually by the architects using models and plans and offered choices on the following:
- gas or electric heating
- position of radiators
- position of electric wall sockets
- layout of kitchen
- colours of kitchen units, bath suites, kitchen and bath floors, type of units, worktops,
- decorated or undecorated walls
- variations on sunspaces (Phase 3 only)
- variation on dining space/kitchen space (Phase 3 only)
- other particular requirements

A recent tenant survey showed 98% satisfaction with the accommodation.

Tenant Participation: a strong tenants' committee met fortnightly with the design team to progress design ideas. Meetings were also arranged with groups of tenants from each communal close to determine communal finishes.

Other Relevant Aspects

The Site

Biodiversity, modification of micro-climate

Indigenous trees and planting reinforced by fencing and low walls have helped to create good wind drag around the site and partially protected entrances. Private garden areas were created at ground level to encourage tenants to maintain the landscaping.

Sustainable and non-toxic materials

An environmental specification which sourced sustainable and non-toxic materials included the following:

- genuine natural water based paints and stains (low toxicity)
- linoleum floor finish from a Scottish factory (reducing transport and low toxicity)
- wood framed windows
- solid wood entrance doors
- natural clay drainage
- no timber preservative treatment inside dwellings
- solid wood skirtings, cill boards and linings instead of mdf

Costs and Maintenance

There have been some problems obtaining adequate servicing for the condensing boilers and high maintenance costs associated with having to re-paint the external overcladding every few years. Costs were within Scottish Homes standard cost yardsticks. 90% HAG funding was obtained.

Figure 9.2 The flats before conversion in phases 2 and 3

Figure 9.3 The flats after conversion showing infilled balconies to create sunspaces.

Figure 9.4 Phase 1 allowed tenants to cultivate their own gardens for the first time and provided good sheltering at ground level.

Case Study No.10
Self Build, Low Embodied Energy

Link Housing Association, Benarty Self-Builders, Fife

Type:	Newbuild, self-build, shared ownership 1/2 storey
Number of units:	5

SAP rating:	96
U-values:	0.16 Wm^{2}C roof
	0.22 Wm^{2}C walls
	0.16 Wm^{2}C floor
Fuel costs:	n/a

Works costs:	£160,000 total (excludes sweat equity)
Unit cost:	£32,000

Completion date:	April 2000

Contacts:	**Client:**	Link Housing Association	John McDowall	0131 557 0350
	Architect:	Duncan Roberts Architect	Duncan Roberts	01668 213146
	Builder:	Benarty Self Build Housing Association		
	Project Manager	Community Self Buid Scotland	Robert Chalmers	0131 443 7081

This scheme demonstrates the contribution to social housing that collective self-build can make, providing construction skills for a local community and reinforcing the local economy. The brownfield site chosen is within an existing interwar housing estate a few miles outside Glenrothes. Local amenities are 400 yards away. Car parking is in curtilage as per planning requirements of two spaces per house.

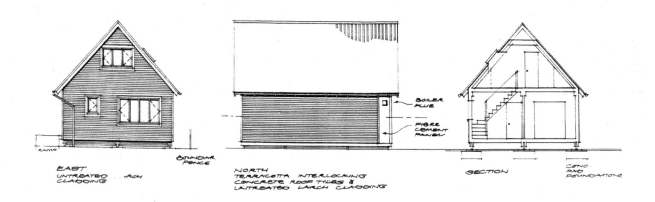

Figure 10.1 Elevation and section of two storey self-build house showing the economy of "room in the roof" timber construction (drawing by Duncan Roberts).

Key Features

Social and Management

Self-build, tenant training, avoiding wet trades, gender balance

Self-build is sometimes treated with caution by housing providers because of perceived additional management requirements. In this case, the partnership with CSBS has minimised any additional requirements.

Tenant training: the housing association formed a partnership with Community Self Build Scotland (CSBS), a specialist support agency for social housing self-builders. Funding was provided by Scottish Homes, the Scottish Executive and the European Social Fund. A group of unemployed residents from the local area who wished to build their own homes was formed and they received training at Lauder College in Dunfermline. A site supervisor and project manager are funded via CSBS to help oversee the work and continue the training.

The quality of workmanship on site is particularly impressive and shows the care and concern that is engendered when building "a home of your own". Wet trades are avoided and the use of lightweight construction built collectively has encouraged women to participate in an area generally reserved for men.

Figure 10.2 The use of lightweight timber construction has encouraged women to take part.

Energy

Low embodied energy, breathing insulation

Wall insulation: 150mm Warmcel cellulose insulation
Loft insulation: 300mm Warmcel cellulose insulation
Floor insulation: 175mm Warmcel cellulose insulation

Embodied energy: the houses are constructed using a timber post and beam method pioneered by Walter Segal[1] which minimises concrete foundations and reduces resources required in the underbuilding. The use of indigenous larch cladding further reduces the embodied energy compared to traditional block construction. This form of construction was particularly appropriate given that the site had poor bearing capacity due to peaty deposits. One drawback, however, is the need for ramps or steps as the ground floor is raised from the ground.

Breathing insulation: the use of cellulose insulation and bitvent sheathing combined with a rainscreen of timber cladding ensures that the walls are "breathing" and allow moisture to diffuse away from the inner surfaces.

Other Relevant Aspects

Healthy Dwellings

Sustainable and non-toxic materials

An environmental specification which sourced sustainable and non-toxic materials included the following:

- wood framed windows
- natural clay drainage
- no timber treatment inside dwellings, apart from exposed internal frame members
- solid wood skirtings, cill boards and linings instead of mdf.

---

[1] Broome and Richardson (1991)

Costs and Maintenance

In recognition of the "sweat equity" put in by the self builders, they get a 25% share in the ownership. Being shared ownership, the residents are wholly responsible for the maintenance of the scheme. As self-builders they will be better equipped for this task than most new owner occupiers. The project forms a good model for housing providers who wish to introduce genuine low-cost ownership into their stock.

Case Study No.11

Embedded Solar Sunspaces, High Insulation

Perthshire Housing Association, Nelson Street, Perth

Type:	New build, solid masonry, 3 and 4 storey flatted
Number of units:	27

SAP rating:	**92**
U-values:	**0.18 Wm^{2}C roof**
	0.25 Wm^{2}C walls
Fuel costs:	**£3-6.23 pw (predicted)**

Works costs:	£1,215,589
Unit cost:	£45,000

Completion date:	August 1997

Contacts:	**Client:**	Perthshire Housing Association	Alison Cook	01738 441088
	Architect:	Milton Studios, Glamis	James F. Stephen	01307 840254
	Builder:	Taycon Construction Ltd, Dundee	R J Cowan	01382 622321

This development of two and four person flats has been designed to achieve high levels of energy efficiency within a traditional solid masonry structure. The intention of the client was to address an increase in the incidence of fuel poverty triggered by the addition of VAT to fuel bills. The scheme is also high density (117 dph) and built on a brownfield site. It is situated in the centre of Perth and is within easy walking distances of local amenities. It is also well served by public transport and has an exceptionally low level of car-parking (6 off-street car spaces only).

Figure 11.1 Solar sunspaces are embedded into this scheme, maximising effciency.

Key Features

Energy Use

High insulation, sunspaces

High energy efficiency is achieved through:

- south-facing sunspaces supplying warm air to the rest of the dwelling
- sun shades to prevent overheating of the sunspaces when the sun is strongest
- increased insulation (walls 80mm styrofoam, roof 200mm mineral fibre, floor 35mm styrofoam)
- low energy windows (low emissivity, argon-filled giving U-value of 1.24).

The sunspaces are embedded into the buildings' structure rather than added on like conservatories and ventilate into the bedroom and living room spaces. Kitchen and bathroom are internal and have no external windows, although a window from the kitchen faces into the sunspace.

The whole building acts as a passive thermal store because it is made of solid masonry. Wet plaster was used on the walls to maximise the efficiency of thermal storage.

Since the development has been occupied there are indications that the combination of extra insulation and sunspaces has increased energy efficiency to such an extent that boilers could have been smaller and central heating may not have been necessary. Radiators were installed in order to address tenants' perceptions of heating requirements rather than the actual heating requirement. This development also demonstrates that the attractiveness of sunspaces can lead occupants to annex them as additional living space with fitted carpets etc which can compromise their effectiveness. This highlights a need for educating the occupier in relation to energy efficiency.

Other Relevant Aspects

Costs and Maintenance

Costs, although within an agreed budget with Scottish Homes, are approximately £10,000 per unit over standard costs. The high cost is attributable more to difficult ground conditions and the need for flood protection than to the higher environmental specification.

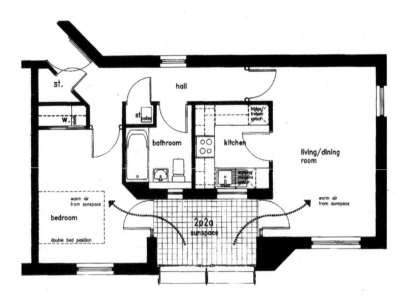

Figure 11.2 The floor plan shows how the sunspace pre-warms the living spaces.

Case Study No.12

Combined Heat and Power (CHP), District Heating and Energy Strategy

Perthshire Housing Association and Servite Housing Association, Scott Street, Perth

Type: **Number of units:**	New build, solid masonry, 3 and 4 storey flatted 33 general needs flats (PHA) plus PHA office accommodation and 30 unit sheltered housing (SHA)
SAP rating: **U-values:** **Fuel costs:**	**n/a and does not allow for district heating or CHP** **0.35 Wm²C roof** **0.45 Wm²C walls** **0.45 Wm²C floor** **£6.18 pw (Servite HA)**
Works costs: **Unit cost:**	£3,500,000 total excluding office fit out £49,795 (Servite HA)　　　　£40,421 (Perthshire HA)
Completion date:	April 1999
Contacts:	**Client:**　Perthshire Housing Association　　Alison Cook　　01738 441088 　　　　　　Servite Housing Association　　Andrew Kirkpatrick　01382 480915 **Architect:**　Keppie Architects　　　　　Geoff Taplin　　01738 631551 **Builder:**　Brown Construction　　　　　C Jolly　　　　01382 739683

This is a mixed-use development by Perthshire Housing Association (PHA) and Servite Housing Association (SHA). The development comprises 33 flats for PHA plus a 30 unit sheltered housing development in a separate but adjacent building for SHA. The buildings are four storey tenements with new offices for Perthshire Housing Association on the ground floor of the PHA building. The development is on a brownfield site and is very central with local amenities immediately adjacent. Parking is well below planning guidance levels and the development is well served by public transport.

Key Features

Energy Use

CHP, District Heating

The sheltered housing was designed to use district heating on a 24 hour basis and a joint development of this scale and diversity of power demands offered an ideal opportunity to install combined heat and power.

The CHP plant is a modified transit van "lean burn" engine which generates electricity using gas instead of petrol. The heat produced by the generator is recovered to heat water. Water is also heated by the district heating system, which consists of a series of boilers in the plant room. Hot water is pumped around the buildings to heat wet radiators in each room. To the tenant the system looks normal other than not having a boiler in the home. The CHP is deliberately undersized to avoid unnecessary surplus in the summer and produces up to 40% of the electricity required, the remaining power and back up in case of failure coming from mains gas and electricity. The use of CHP increases the efficiency of electrical production from 30% (standard power stations) to 85%.

The CHP installation formed a separate specialist contract outwith the main building contract to accommodate the need for a nominated supplier.

Figure 12.1 Rear view of scheme showing gable end flue to CHP plant room.

Benefits

- less pollution through more efficient heat and power generation (CO_2 emissions reduced by 50%)
- lower fuel bills for tenants and the Associations. This is achieved through the CHP and because the Associations can enter into bulk purchase agreements with power suppliers

Perthshire Housing Association are now in negotiation to extend the use of CHP as part of their volume procurement contract for 300 dwellings over 3 years. This will involve partnership with a local hospital, school and housing.

Social and Management

Metering of District Heating, Mixed Use

Running costs for gas and electricity and maintenance costs for the CHP will be recovered from the tenants and PHA office. PHA tenants pay a weekly service charge for heating varied according to size of flat (£3.40 for one bedroom and £4.55 for two bedrooms in 1999). Individual use of hot water and electricity will be metered with each flat fitted with a pre-payment meter. Tenants purchase £5 cards from the office downstairs or from a local shop. Every £5 card buys 100KWhrs of electricity compared to the normal tariff which would buy 56KWhrs. Since PHA is the power supplier it must take responsibility for debt recovery and voids. The use of pre-payment cards minimises the need for management and meter readings.

In Servite's sheltered properties, the tenants pay all fuel charges along with their monthly rent and therefore benefit from costs being spread evenly over the year. A proportion of the cost is identified for common areas and remaining costs vary according to the size of the flat.

Figure 12.2 Front view of the scheme showing mixed use with Perthshire Housing Association offices immediately below the residential accommodation.

A management agreement has been established to determine the duties and responsibilities of the two Associations. Servite manage the CHP and are responsible for the gas supply in order that the two associations can benefit from Servite's ability to procure gas at approximately 35% savings on normal domestic tariffs.

The location of the Perthshire Housing Association offices within the building provides a mixed use development.

Other Relevant Aspects

Costs and Maintenance

Costs are within an agreed budget with Scottish Homes. The CHP plant cost £45,000 in addition to the district heating boiler, pipework and radiators, offset by £17,000 with a grant from Energy Efficiency Standards of Performance. The meters cost £300 to install. The payback on installing the CHP system in terms of reduced energy bills is 3-5 years. Regular maintenance of the CHP plant is essential and costly.

Perthshire Housing Association are currently considering the transfer of the capital cost of future energy efficiency measures to a revenue cost via leasing agreements. Revenue costs can then be recovered by increasing the rents by a proportion of the savings to the tenant from the energy efficiency measures. Servite passes all savings on to the tenants.

Case Study No.13
Car-free Sustainable Housing

Slateford Green, Edinburgh, Canmore Housing Association and Malcolm Homes Ltd

Type:	New build tenement flats
Number of units:	120 (69 rented, 25 Low Cost Home Ownership (LCHO), 26 for sale)

SAP rating:	**96**
U-values:	**0.18 Wm^{2}C roof**
	0.2 Wm^{2}C walls
Fuel costs:	**£17 to £30 per annum depending on location**

Works costs:	Canmore £7.31 million; Malcolm Homes £2.24 million
Unit cost:	Rented/LCHO £77,745
	Owner occupied £86,192

Completion date:	March 2000

Contacts:	**Client:**	Canmore Housing Association and Malcolm Homes Ltd	Graham Harper	0131 623 7378
	Architect:	Hackland and Dore Architects	Alastair Hackland	0131 538 7707
	Builder:	Hart Builders (Edinburgh) Ltd		01875 610891

Key features

Slateford Green is an innovative development exhibiting many sustainability features, including:

- car-free
- brownfield site
- mixed tenure
- materials with minimal environmental impact
- super insulation
- passive stack ventilation

Car-free

Slateford Green is built on the former railway goods yard at Gorgie, close to Haymarket and with good access to many facilities and public transport. It is thus an ideal site for a car-free residential development. The space that would have been devoted to parking spaces has instead been used for gardens, children's play areas and allotments. Car ownership levels among Canmore's tenants as a whole are less than 20%, and the involvement of Malcolm Homes to produce a mixed tenure development not only provides a socially balanced community but also demonstrates the financial viability of housing for sale that is car-free and incorporates sustainable construction methods.

A Section 75 agreement under the Town and Country Planning (Scotland) Act 1997 requires Canmore to impose obligations in each tenancy agreement by which the tenant will undertake not to park any vehicle within the development. Complementary to the development is the City Car Club, a joint venture by Edinburgh City Council and Budget Car Rental. Already operational elsewhere in Edinburgh, Slateford Green will be the second site in the city. For an annual fee, members of the club have access to a fleet of vehicles which can be hired locally by the hour.

Scheme Design

A design competition was won by Hackland and Dore of Edinburgh. The design is derived from the traditional Edinburgh tenement block, with its sheltered courtyard form adapted to the site and maximizing solar gain. There are 120 flats and a community hall within a 2-4 storey perimeter block. The block encloses terraced gardens and is surrounded by natural landscape and allotments. No vehicles enter the courtyard and minimal parking is available for people with disabilities and essential visitors.

Figure 13.1 An illustration of the scheme showing car-free space within the block.

The construction is lightweight dry-fix with reduced costs through prefabrication and waste reduction. Materials have been sourced for minimal environmental impact, reduced maintenance and their capacity for recycling.

Energy

Energy saving is achieved mainly by super insulation. The structure is clad with a breathing wall with 175mm of Warmcel with panel-vent sheathing. Most flats have conservatories providing passive solar gain to living spaces orientated into the south-facing courtyard. The intention had been to incorporate a district heating system, the primary heat source being reject condensate from the nearby North British Distillery, available at low cost. However, legal obstacles meant that this had to be abandoned in favour of the gas-fired boilers serving each stair which were originally intended only to provide back-up.

Natural ventilation is encouraged by passive stack ventilation and there is provision for retrofitting of photovoltaic panels to power lighting if and when practical cost effective products become available.

Guildford College
Learning Resource Centre

Please return on or before the last date shown.
No further issues or renewals if any items are overdue.
"7 Day" loans are **NOT** renewable.

1 0 FEB 2005

0 3 MAR 2005

2 3 FEB 2006

2 3 APR 2010

Class: _720.472 STE_

Title: _SUSTAINABLE HOUSING DESIGN_

Author: _STEVENSON, Fionn_

Printed in the United Kingdom for The Stationery Office.
TJ002312, C10, 9/00, 5673